P9-CBT-828

CRAFT

A Handbook for Teachers of Intermediate Art

AUTHOR
MARY E. PLATTS
WITH PHOTOGRAPHS BY
GIL MASTERS

PUBLISHED BY
EDUCATIONAL SERVICE, INC.
P.O. Box 219
Stevensville, Michigan 49127

Copyright 1977©
EDUCATIONAL SERVICE, INC.
P. O. Box 219
Stevensville, Michigan 49127
Printed in U.S.A.
ISBN #89273-124-9

TABLE OF CONTENTS

*Shown In Photographs On Designated Page

*Shown In Photographs On Designated Page

*Shown In Photographs On Designated Page

*Shown In Photographs On Designated Page

INTRODUCTION

CRAFTS presents a wide variety of fresh, creative ideas for classroom art activities. Projects are included to appeal to a great range of interests and to suit highly varying levels of ability.

Materials used are inexpensive (many are free) and easily obtained. Directions are concise and easy to follow. All activities have been tested and we include cautions to help you avoid whatever problems and/or failures we experienced during this testing process. Examples of most projects are shown in photographs to give you a precise concept of how the finished work will look. Every effort has been made to make this a truly functional, easy-to-use handbook of ideas for arts and crafts activities.

Art is unique among all subjects in the school curriculum. Every child loves it! Teachers have no problems stimulating interest — children are eager and enthusiastic. The problem is what to do for art today. Thumb through the pages of CRAFT. We hope we have helped you solve that problem.

SECTION I:

"A Splash Of Color, A Dash Of Design"

Bright colors and bold designs for classroom art projects.

TOP ROW: Bubble Name Designs, Circle Cut-Outs
CENTER ROW: Triple Exposure (2 examples)
BOTTOM ROW: Quilt Block Design, Tri-Color

1. BUBBLE LETTER DESIGNS (Shown on page 3, upper left)

A. Materials: Provide white paper, pencil, felt pens in a variety of colors (crayons could be used if desired), scissors, glue and colored construction paper.

B. Procedure: This is an excellent get-acquainted activity to use at the beginning of the school year. Ask each student to write his name in bubble letters on white paper. (Use pencil for this initial step so errors in design can be erased and corrected.)

First, make the initial letter in a stylized block form as shown in figure 1. The second letter should look partially tucked behind the first letter as shown in figure 2. Each successive letter should look partially tucked behind the previous one as shown in figure 3.

Example:

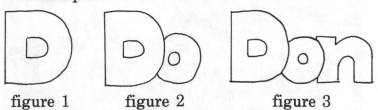

figure 1   figure 2   figure 3

Trace around the borders of each letter with a dark colored felt pen. Then, use a variety of colors to texture each letter. For example, the first letter could be peppered with blue dots, the next filled with yellow stripes, the next with green zig-zag lines and so on.

Cut out the finished design as a single, complete unit — do not cut apart individual letters. Mount it on a sheet of construction paper for display.

2. CIRCLE CUT-OUTS (Shown on page 3, upper right)

A. Materials: Students will need construction paper in several coordinating colors (blues and greens, or a red/orange/yellow combination, etc.), white mounting sheets, scissors, glue, pencil, paper punch and spools or other round objects to use for tracing circle shapes.

B. Procedure: Trace closely-shaped circles on construction paper scraps of several harmonizing colors. Cut out the circles. From the remaining border scraps, punch many holes at random with a paper punch.

Arrange the cut-out circles and border scraps on the white mounting sheet to form an interesting abstract pattern. The tiny circles cut by the paper punch can be scattered among the design if desired.

Make many trial arrangements until you find one that pleases you. Then, lift up one shape at a time, apply glue to the back and set it in place. Continue in this way until all the shapes are glued into place.

3. TRIPLE EXPOSURE (2 examples shown on page 3, center)

A. Materials: Provide white paper, felt pens (or crayons) in three shades of the same color (for example, pale, medium and dark blue). You will also need a shape to trace. (In the photograph on page 3, one design was made by tracing the shape of a pair of opened scissors. The other was traced around an apple slicer.) If preferred, an interesting shape can be cut from lightweight cardboard to use as the tracing pattern.

B. Procedure: Lay the shape in the center of the paper. Use the medium color pen to trace its shape. Move the shape to the right so it overlaps the center tracing halfway. Use the palest color to trace its shape. Move the shape to the far left so it overlaps the center tracing halfway. Use the darkest color to trace its shape.

The resulting pattern looks like a triple-exposed picture. It makes you look twice!

4. QUILT BLOCK DESIGNS (Shown on page 3, lower left)

A. Materials: Students will need scraps of gift wrapping paper in a wide variety of colors and patterns, scissors, glue and white or colored paper to be used as mounting sheets.

For making patterns, you will need scrap paper, pencils, ruler and/or compass. If desired, have library books on display showing traditional quilt block patterns so children will have some idea of the many creative arrangement possibilities.

B. Procedure: Cut squares, circles, diamonds, triangles, etc., from scrap paper and make trial arrangements of the pieces to form a pleasing "Quilt Block Design."

When you are satisfied with your arrangement, use these scrap paper pieces as patterns and cut the shapes out of gift wrapping paper of a color and design of your choice. Arrange the colored pieces on a sheet of construction paper, duplicating your trial arrangement. Lift one piece at a time, place a few drops of glue along the backside margin and press it into place. Continue in this way gluing down all pieces of the "Quilt Block Design."

5. TRI-COLORS (Shown on page 3, lower right)

A. Materials: Provide white paper, pencil and colored felt pens or crayons.

B. Procedure: With a pencil, very lightly draw free form shapes all over the paper (overlapping the shapes as you draw, see figure 1). Completely fill the paper with these overlapping shapes.

Example:

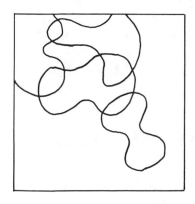

figure 1
Partially Com-
pleted Design

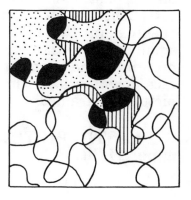

figure 2
Design Completed,
Coloring Partially
Completed

Choose three colors closely related on the color wheel (such as red/orange/yellow, or blue/green/purple) or three shades of the same color (such as pale, medium and dark blue). Use these three colors to fill in all areas of the design, one color for each separate area (see figure 2).

6. PAPER CUTTER ART (Shown on page 9, upper left and center)

A. Materials: Students will need construction paper in black and many other colors, mounting sheets, paper cutter, scissors and glue.

B. Procedure: Cut strips of varying widths, squares and/or rectangles of colored construction paper. (Use a paper cutter to make this work go quickly.)

Assemble the pieces on a mounting sheet to form a pleasing pattern, then glue them in place.

To make a frame, lay the completed picture on black construction paper. Trace its shape, then cut about 1/4 inch inside this line to make an opening in the black paper that is slightly smaller than the picture. Apply glue to the margin of the frame opening and lay the picture face down onto it. Turn it over and there is the picture all framed!

7. PLASTIC PICTURES (Shown on page 9, upper right)

A. Materials: Provide plastic berry baskets (used for packaging berries, cherry tomatoes, mushrooms, etc., in produce markets), scissors, white glue and tagboard mounting sheets.

B. Procedure: Look closely at the patterns in the plastic basket. Use scissors to cut the basket into flat pieces with interesting geometric shapes. Make many trial arrangements of these pieces on the mounting sheet, fitting them together to form one large geometric design.

When you have an arrangement that pleases you, lift one piece at a time, put a few drops of glue on the back and set it back into place. Con-

TOP ROW: Paper Cutter Art (2 examples), Plastic Pictures
CENTER ROW: Burlap Distortion, Rainbow Contour
BOTTOM ROW: Abstracts (2 examples)

tinue in this way until all pieces are glued in place. Gently lay a book on top of the arrangement to hold the plastic pieces firmly in the glue until the glue dries.

C. Variation: After pieces are cut, lay them on a newspaper and spray them with enamel paint of any color. (The pieces used in the arrangement shown on page 9 were sprayed with high gloss black enamel.) When the paint is thoroughly dry, arrange and glue the pieces as previously described.

8. BURLAP DISTORTIONS (Shown on page 9, center left)

A. Materials: Burlap, scissors, glue and white or colored paper to be used as mounting sheets are needed for this activity.

B. Procedure: Cut a shape (square, circle, oval, rectangle, etc.) from burlap. Pull many vertical and horizontal threads from the burlap. Stretch and pull the burlap out of its original shape. Push some threads close together and pull others far apart. Put your fingers into open places and stretch the openings larger.

When the entire form creates a pleasing design, apply a few drops of glue here and there to the back of the burlap and place it on the mounting sheet. You may wish to set a book on top of the work to keep it flat while the glue dries.

9. RAINBOW CONTOURS (Shown on page 9, center right)

A. Materials: Students will need paper and pencil. The designs may be colored with felt pens, crayons, water colors or tempera paints.

B. Procedure: Use a pencil to draw one wavy or jagged line all the way across the paper. Above this, spaced closely to the first or far away, draw a second line following the same contours as the first line. Continue drawing more contour lines, spacing some close together and others far apart until the entire paper is filled with contour lines.

Use crayons, felt pens, water colors or tempera paints to color the stripes in a wide variety of colors.

10. ABSTRACTS (Shown on page 9, bottom row)

A. Materials: Provide tagboard or smooth-surfaced white paper, black felt pens and household items in a variety of shapes.

In the photograph on page 9, the example on the left was made by tracing the shapes of a wooden spoon, teaspoon and scissors. The example on the right used the shape of a kitchen spatula. Round jar lids, rectangular spice cans, flat sticks or stones of irregular shapes, etc., could be used.

B. Procedure: Place one object on the paper and use a black felt pen to trace its shape. Move the same object to a new place and trace its shape again. Move the same object so it overlaps the shapes you have already drawn and trace its shape again. Continue in this manner using one or several objects for tracing until you have completed a design of overlapping shapes. Then, use a felt pen to color every other space black.

C. Variations:

1. Instead of using solid black and white, areas can be textured in various ways. Put straight or wavy lines in some areas, dots in others and so forth. Color some areas solid black and leave some white for contrast.

2. For a dizzying effect, use an optically vibrating combination of colors for these designs. (See The Use Of Color In Op Art, page 213.) For example, use a bright green felt pen on bright red paper or a bright green and blue color combination.

11. PERSONALITY COLLAGE (Shown on page 13, upper left)

A. Materials: Old magazines, scissors, glue and mounting sheets are needed for this activity.

B. Procedure: This is an excellent get-acquainted activity to use at the beginning of the school year. Look through old magazines for pictures that show your personal interests. You may find pictures of your favorite sports, foods, pets, hobbies, career interests or any other things that you like. Cut out these pictures and arrange them to overlap and completely cover the mounting sheet. Glue each picture in place.

Find headline-sized letters in the magazines to spell your name. Glue your name anywhere on the arrangement.

12. GRAPHIC COLLAGE (Shown on page 13, upper right)

A. Materials: Students will need old magazines, scissors, glue and white paper.

TOP ROW: Personality Collage, Graphic Collage
CENTER ROW: Texture Collage, Theme Collage
BOTTOM ROW: Surrealistic Collages (2 examples)

B. Procedure: Cut black and white headline-sized letters from old magazines. You may cut complete words or letter combinations of a pleasing design. Cut some letters that are printed black on a white background and a few printed white on a black background for contrast.

Make trial arrangements of the letters on the white mounting sheet. When the overall pattern pleases you, lift one piece at a time, apply glue to the back and press it into place. Continue in this way until all parts are glued down.

The final collage does not say anything. The pattern of letters simply forms a pleasing graphic design.

13. TEXTURE COLLAGE (Shown on page 13, center left)

A. Materials: Provide old magazines, scissors, glue and paper for mounting the arrangements.

B. Procedure: Look through old magazines for pictures showing interesting texture designs. You might find zig-zag tire tread designs, fuzzy carpet patterns, rough wood paneling, wind blown grass or weeds, jagged rocks, smooth water, soft hair — any designs showing variety and contrast in texture.

Cut out sections of these patterns. Arrange them in a pleasing design and glue them onto the mounting sheet to create a "Texture Collage."

14. THEME COLLAGE (Shown on page 13, center right)

A. Materials: Old magazines, scissors, glue and paper are needed for this activity.

B. Procedure: Cut colored pictures of a great many objects of one category from old magazines. For example, cut all pictures of cars, eyes or fruit, or sports players in action. Arrange the pictures to overlap and completely cover the mounting sheet, then glue them in place.

15. SURREALISTIC COLLAGE (Shown on page 13, lower row)

A. Materials: Students will need old magazines, scissors, glue and paper for mounting the pictures.

B. Procedure: Cut pictures from magazines and assemble them to form a picture. While each picture used in the arrangement is totally normal and realistic, the combination of pictures should form a scene that is absurd, surprising or downright shocking.

Look at the two examples shown on page 13. In the left-hand picture, fashion models pose for the photographer, which is totally normal. But, look closely. Each model has the head of an animal.

The right-hand example derives its surprise from the scale of the pictures used. A close-up picture of a lizard combined with a long-distance shot of hikers makes the lizard appear to be a dinosaur-sized beast stalking its prey.

Here are a few more ideas. Find a close-up picture of a plate of spaghetti. Cut slits here and there in the picture. In each slit, tuck the head of a person so it looks like a group of people are submerged nose-deep in the spaghetti.

Cut out the picture of a laughing baby. Surround the baby with cut-out flowers so the scene is one of total sweetness and beauty. Now add the shocker. Give the baby a hideous plaything — a snake, tarantula, etc. Got the idea? Absurdity. Surprise. Downright shock. (If children respond well to this project, they would also enjoy "Surrealistic Arrangements," page 69.)

16. RUBBINGS (Shown on page 17, top row)

A. **Materials:** The paper used for rubbings should be smooth, not too thick and strong enough so it will not tear easily. (Inexpensive, thin typing paper works well.) While a black crayon is the color traditionally used for rubbings, there is no reason why other colors could not be used. However, dark colors will show the print more effectively than light colors. Other miscellaneous materials are needed as described.

B. **Procedure:** Peel the paper off the crayon. Prints are made by rubbing the entire side of the crayon across the paper. Lay the paper over any textured object. Rub across this sheet of paper with the side of the crayon and the texture pattern will appear on the sheet. (It may be easier if one child uses two hands to hold the paper so it will not shift position while another child does the rubbing.)

In the photograph on page 17, the right-hand example was made by rubbing over paper clips laid on wire mesh.

Here are a variety of suggestions for rubbings:

1. Lay paper over textured objects found around the school, such as decorative iron grillwork, bricks, a manhole cover, an artistic mosa-

TOP ROW: Rubbings (2 examples)
CENTER ROW: Patterns of 5, Filagree, Accidental Arrangement
BOTTOM ROW: Bleach Picture, On-Edge Print

ic tile design, highly textured drapery fabric, etc., and make a rubbing of its design.

2. Fold a sheet of paper in haphazard ways. Various portions of the sheet will be one, two or three thicknesses. Lay paper over this folded sheet and make a rubbing. The rubbing will show all fold lines plus the variety of thicknesses (the thickest area will appear dark colored, the thinnest areas pale colored).

3. Cut pieces of construction paper or lightweight tagboard and assemble them to form a realistic or abstract design. Lightly glue them to a backing sheet so they will not shift position. Lay paper over the design and make a rubbing.

4. Cut pieces of construction paper or lightweight tagboard and assemble them to form a realistic or abstract design as described in #3. Cut decorative pieces from construction paper and glue them onto these shapes. The design is now a single layer thick in some areas and two or three thicknesses of paper in others. Lay paper over this design and make a rubbing. The rubbing will appear darkest where the paper is thickest.

5. Cut any basic geometric shape, such as a circle. Cut slits from the margin towards the center. Do not cut all the way to the center (see

Example:

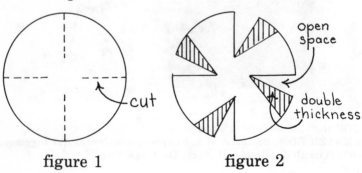

figure 1   figure 2

figure 1). Fold the paper back along each slit (see figure 2). A rubbing of this design will show the double thickness darkest, the single thickness paler and the open spaces palest of all.

6. Use a pen knife or single-edged razor blade to cut shapes from construction paper. One side of each shape must be left attached to the main sheet (see figure 1). Fold back each cut shape to create double thicknesses of paper in some areas and open holes in others (see figure 2). Lay paper over this design and make a rubbing. The double thicknesses will appear darkest, the open holes palest.

Example:

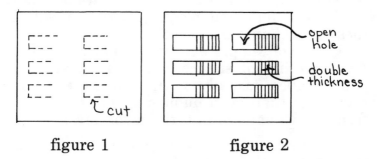

figure 1   figure 2

7. Make an arrangement of textured objects such as paper clips, coils of yarn or string, pieces cut from paper lace doilies or sandpaper, etc. Glue the pieces to a backing sheet so they will not shift position. Lay paper over the arrangement and make a rubbing of its pattern.

17. PATTERNS OF 5 (Shown on page 17, center row, left)

A. Materials: Two contrasting colors of construction paper, scissors or paper cutter and glue are needed for this activity.

Cut many identical shapes from one color of construction paper. Cut all strips, all triangles, all squares, etc. Give each child five of these shapes.

The other color paper will be used for the mounting sheets. If the shapes are small, cut mounting sheets in small sizes so the design will be in proportion to its background. Give each child one mounting sheet.

B. Procedure: Make many trial arrangements of the five shapes on the mounting sheet. When you form a pattern that pleases you, glue the shapes onto the mounting sheet.

When all your patterns are displayed on the bulletin board, you will be amazed at how many totally different and pleasing arrangements of these five shapes are possible.

This is a simple exercise in pattern design. Any quantity of shapes can be used, although odd numbers usually form into more artistic groupings than even numbers. Children tend to form even numbers into right, formal blocks.

C. Variation: This exercise can be used many times. If five strips are used one time, use seven triangles the next time, nine squares another time and so on.

18. FILAGREES (Shown on page 17, center of center row)

A. Materials: Provide black construction paper, pencil, scissors and glue. Designs can be mounted on a variety of colored papers as described in Part B.

B. Procedure: Fold black construction paper in half length-wise. Draw a free-form design along the fold (see figure 1). Draw cut-out "windows" within the design (see figure 2). With paper still folded, cut out the outline and the "window" sections of the design. The result is a black frame resembling that of a stained glass window (see figure 3).

Example:

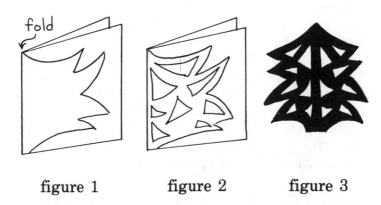

| figure 1 | figure 2 | figure 3 |

Glue the black frame onto colored paper. The example photographed on page 17 was glued onto a colored page cut from an old magazine. It could be glued onto colored tissue paper, construction paper or patterned gift wrap if desired.

Cut away the margins of the colored paper so none shows beyond the borders of the black frame. Mount the completed design on light colored paper for bulletin board display.

19. ACCIDENTAL ARRANGEMENTS
(Shown on page 17, center right)

A. Materials: Construction paper in two contrasting colors, scissors or paper cutter and glue are needed for this activity. (A compass and/or ruler may be needed for creating shapes.)

B. Procedure: Select one sheet of construction paper for a background color. Choose a contrasting or harmonizing color for the design pieces.

Cut 5 - 11 (depending on size) shapes from the second color of paper. The shapes should be identical to each other. They could all be circles, rectangles, narrow strips, free-form designs or whatever you choose. Cut one shape and then use it as a pattern for cutting the remaining shapes.

Hold the set of shapes up above the mounting sheet and simply drop them one at a time, or several at once, onto the paper. Drop them over and over again until they form a pattern that pleases you. Then, lift one shape at a time, apply glue and put it back in place. Continue in this way until all the shapes are glued in place.

20. COLOR SUBTRACTION (Shown on page 17, lower left)

A. Materials: Students will need colored construction paper, liquid household bleach, paintbrushes, teaspoons and colored felt pens. Pour small quantities of bleach into small containers for children's use.

SAFETY PRECAUTION: Household bleach is a caustic poison. Read all cautions on the label. Caution children in extremely careful use of the bleach. Spills on clothing will cause permanent white bleached areas. If any child behaves irresponsibly with these materials, excuse him from further participation in this activity immediately.

B. Procedure: Use a paintbrush to spread a few strokes or blotches of bleach onto the sheet of colored construction paper. Watch what happens. Instead of painting color on, you have taken the color off! Try dripping bleach from a teaspoon onto the paper. This creates a totally new type of pattern.

Study the area bleached of color. Does it remind you of anything? Does it look like a bouquet of flowers, a forest scene, a field of weeds, a fish or butterfly? Bleach out further areas of color if needed. Use a felt pen to add a few quick strokes of color to highlight the picture you see.

21. ON-EDGE PRINTS (Shown on page 17, lower right)

A. Materials: Thin, flexible cardboard (tagboard, shirt cardboard, etc.), tempera paints, brushes and white drawing paper are needed for this activity.

B. Procedure: Paint the edge of the cardboard with tempera paint. Flex the cardboard to form an interesting curved pattern. Press it onto the white drawing paper to print its design.

Use the same cardboard repainted with the same color, flexed in the same or a new way, for further printing. If more than one color is needed, use a separate edge of the cardboard for each color.

22. CARDBOARD PRINTS (Shown on page 24, upper left)

A. Materials: Provide thin cardboard (tagboard, shirt cardboard, etc.), scissors, pencil, glue, tempera paints, brushes and white drawing paper.

TOP ROW: Cardboard Print, Half Portraits
CENTER ROW: Black and White Reflections, Shadows
BOTTOM ROW: Spacemen Have Landed, Typewriter Art (2 examples)

B. Procedure: On a whole sheet of cardboard, use a pencil to draw the outline of the desired picture or design (see figure 1). Cut pieces from a second sheet of cardboard and glue them inside the penciled outlines. Leave a small space between each glued piece (see figure 2).

The lion print shown on page 24 was made from 24 separate cardboard pieces.

Example:

figure 1   figure 2

Brush over the raised design pieces with tempera paint. Lay a sheet of white paper over the design and press with finger tips to transfer the pattern onto the white paper. Lift the print off and set it aside to dry. Repaint the raised cardboard design and press on another sheet of paper to make a second printing. Repeat to make as many prints as desired. (This is a good method for producing designs in quantity, useful as greeting cards, school program covers, etc.)

23. HALF PORTRAITS (Shown on page 24, upper right)

A. Materials: Black and white portraits cut from old magazines or newspapers, glue, scissors, white drawing paper and pencils are needed for this activity.

B. Procedure: This project is exceptionally delightful because it not only produces startlingly effective results, but also totally amazes each child to discover his own skill.

Cut a portrait in half vertically. (The cut should run through the center of the face.) Glue the left portion of the picture onto white drawing paper. (Left handed children should paste on the right portion to make the work easier for them.) Then, use a pencil to sketch on the drawing paper the missing half of the face, duplicating the printed half as closely as possible. First, draw the basic outline, then sketch in details and finally add shading as needed.

Let each child do several portraits. They are quick to do and provide excellent practice in sketching and shading facial portraits. Each successive sketch will show progressively greater skill.

24. BLACK AND WHITE REFLECTIONS
(Shown on page 24, center left)

A. Materials: Each child will need a full sheet of white construction paper, a half-sheet of black construction paper, scissors and glue.

B. Procedure: For best understanding of this concept, study the photograph on page 24. Pieces were cut away from the half-sheet of black paper. Then, the border of the black paper was glued onto the right side of the white paper. All the cut-away black pieces were glued onto the left side of the white paper to form an exact reflection with the color scheme reversed.

25. SHADOWS (Shown on page 24, center right)

A. Materials: You will need a sunny day, hard surfaced paper (ink absorbs into porous paper making lines appear fuzzy), pencil and felt pens.

B. Procedure: Go outdoors on a sunny day and look for interesting shadow designs. The beauty of shadow patterns cast by the most common of objects may surprise you. The photograph on page 24 shows the shadow of a bicycle wheel. Look at the shadows of a chain link fence, a tree branch, the bars of a jungle gym. The angle of the sun often distorts the shadow and makes it elongated or more squat than the original object, which adds to the artistic interest.

Lay the paper on the ground so the shadow is cast upon it and use a pencil to lightly trace the pattern. Then, go inside so you can work on a flat table surface. Use a felt pen to trace over the design, filling in solid areas so the pattern appears as a silhouette. Use a ruler to guide lines that should be perfectly straight (such as the bicycle spokes). When the ink is thoroughly dry, erase all penciled guidelines that show.

The example photographed on page 24 was done in black and white, but color could be used effectively. Two shades of one color work very well. For example, use dark blue ink on light blue paper or purple ink on lavendar paper.

26. SPACEMEN HAVE LANDED (Shown on page 24, lower left)

A. Materials: Students will need tagboard, a medicine dropper, tempera paint (or drawing ink) and old newspapers.

B. Procedure: Cut tagboard sheets approximately 4 by 6 inches (10 by 15 cm) in size. (These designs are small and would look out of scale on larger paper.) Spread newspapers on the floor for protection against paint splashes. Place the tagboard on the papers, leaning it against a chair or table leg so it stands at a slant.

Put thinly mixed tempera paint or drawing ink into the medicine dropper. From approximately waist height, drop paint drops one by one onto the tagboard. Each drop will form a blob where it strikes the tagboard and spidery "legs" as the paint runs downhill. The shapes resemble imaginary creatures from outer space. If the tagboard is leaned almost upright, the paint will run freely creating slender "spaceman" shapes with long, gangly legs. Leaning the paper at a less severe slant will create fat "spaceman" shapes with shorter legs.

Experiment by dropping paint drops onto the paper leaned at various degrees of slant to produce your favorite style of "spaceman."

27. TYPEWRITER ART (Two examples of negative stencils are shown on page 24, lower center and right.)

A. Materials: You will need a typewriter and typing paper, scissors, pencil and rubber cement. For the graph designed pictures, graph paper is also needed. Provide correction tape or correction fluid and show children how to use it. (If children have to start all over again each time they type an error, most will grow discouraged long before the project is complete.)

Probably all children in the classroom will need to share one typewriter. Explain and demonstrate the procedure to the class and have children prepare their stencils or graph designs as a group. Set up the typewriter in a corner of the classroom or out in the hall where the noise will not disturb the class. Let children take turns using the machine to complete their pictures.

B. Procedure:

1. Positive Stencils: On one sheet of typing paper, draw a simple silhouette-type design. Cut out the design and discard it. The margin section of this paper will be used as the stencil.

Spread a few small areas of rubber cement on the back of the stencil and fasten it onto a second sheet of typing paper. Put this into the typewriter and, beginning at the top of the cut-out section, simply type single spaced rows of identical characters until you reach the lowest part of the cut-out design. Any characters typed outside the "hole" of the stencil will appear on the stencil margins, not on the whole sheet below it. Carefully peel the stencil from the whole sheet and use your fingers to rub away any remaining rubber cement. The exact shape of the cut-away portion of the stencil is now reproduced in a solid block of typewriter characters on the whole sheet of paper.

2. Negative Stencils: Cut a simple silhouette-type shape from typing paper (as directed in #1) but this time discard the margin section of the paper and cement the shape itself onto a second, whole sheet of typing paper. Set typewriter margins at least five spaces beyond the right and left edges of the stencil design. Beginning at least five rows above the top margin of the stencil, type rows of single spaced identical characters across the entire sheet. Type right over the top of the stencil piece as you go. Continue typing at least five rows below the bottom edge of the stencil design. Peel away the stencil piece and rub off any remaining rubber cement. The design will stand out in white against a dark background of typewritten characters.

3. **Graphed Designs:** On graph paper, mark X's in squares to create the desired design. (These designs can be much more intricate than those previously described.) Each square on the graph represents one typewriter space. Put a clean sheet of typing paper into the typewriter. Follow the design one row at a time, typing a character in a space or skipping that space to leave it blank, according to the graphed plan.

28. GLUE-RUN DESIGNS (Shown on page 31, upper left)

A. Materials: Provide white tagboard, white glue in a squeeze-top bottle, black India ink, paintbrushes and old newspapers. You will also need a sanding block. (Simply wrap sandpaper around a block of wood and nail or tape it securely in place. This keeps the sandpaper perfectly flat during use.)

B. Procedure: Protect the work surface from spills by covering it with a layer of old newspapers. Hold the tagboard at an almost upright angle. Squeeze a thick line of glue along the top

TOP ROW: Glue-Run Design, Tissue Overlay
LOWER LEFT: Strips, Strips, Strips (2 examples)
LOWER RIGHT: Gold and Enamel Designs (2 examples)

of the tagboard, allowing the glue to run down the paper in a series of dribble lines. Add more lines of glue below the first if the pattern looks incomplete. (The example shown on page 31 used four separate pourings to complete the design.) Lay the tagboard flat and allow the glue to dry thoroughly. Then, brush a coat of black India ink across the entire sheet. When the ink is thoroughly dry, rub over the surface of the paper with a sanding block. This will remove ink from the high ridges of glue allowing the design to show clearly in white against a black background.

29. TISSUE OVERLAY (Shown on page 31, upper right)

A. Materials: Tissue paper in a variety of colors, scissors, plain paper to use as a mounting sheet and rubber cement are needed for this activity. (Other adhesives could be used, but rubber cement causes the least warping and color bleed of the tissue paper.)

B. Procedure: Cut pieces from colored tissue paper and use rubber cement to fasten them onto the mounting sheet to form any desired realistic picture or abstract design. Use a variety of colors and allow shapes to overlap to form interesting color blends.

Use the rubber cement very sparingly — just enough to hold each piece in place. Too much cement will cause the paper to warp from the dampness and the colors will also bleed.

30. STRIPS, STRIPS, STRIPS (2 examples shown on page 31, left center and lower left)

A. Materials: Paper for mounting the designs, scissors and glue are needed for this activity. Strips may be cut from a wide variety of materials; such as, construction paper, newspaper, brown grocery bags, aluminum foil, tissue paper, fabric, patterned gift wrap, ribbon, yarn, string, etc.

B. Procedure: Cut strips of various widths from any of the materials suggested selecting colors and patterns that go well together. Use strips cut from a variety of materials to achieve interesting color and texture variations.

Make many trial arrangements of the strips on the mounting sheet. Strips should be placed tightly side by side to completely cover the mounting sheet. When an arrangement pleases you, lift one strip at a time, apply glue to the back and press it back into place. Continue in this way gluing all strips in place. When the glue is thoroughly dry, trim the ends of any strips that extend beyond the margins of the mounting sheet.

31. GOLD AND ENAMEL PICTURES (2 examples shown on page 31, right center and lower right)

A. Materials: Students will need tagboard, pencil, ruler and/or compass, white glue, gold gift-wrap cord, high-gloss enamel paints, small paintbrushes and solvent for cleaning brushes.

SAFETY PRECAUTION: Because the fumes, as well as the liquid paint and solvent, are highly flammable, work outdoors if possible. If working indoors, make sure there is good ventilation and there is no open flame nor electric heating units operating in the room.

B. Procedure: Draw a simple abstract or realistic pattern with pencil on the tagboard. Use a compass or ruler as needed. Lay a thin line of glue along each penciled line. Lay gold gift-wrap cord along these lines of glue, pressing it firmly into the glue. Allow the glue to dry thoroughly. Spread a protective layer of old newspapers over the work surface. Then, paint each area of the design with high-gloss enamel paint. Use one color per area, but different areas can be various harmonizing colors. Try not to get paint on the gold cord. Allow paint to dry thoroughly before handling the pictures. Clean all brushes immediately with paint solvent.

32. SPLASH STARBURSTS (Shown on page 35, left)

A. Materials: Provide old newspapers, tagboard, drawing ink in two highly contrasting colors, a paintbrush and a medicine dropper.

B. Procedure: Spread newspapers on the floor to protect against ink spills. Cut tagboard into 6 inch (15 cm) squares. (These designs are small and would look out of scale on large paper.) Read through the following directions before beginning to work. Once you begin, you must work quickly before the ink has time to dry.

Fill the medicine dropper with drawing ink and set it where it is handy for quick use. Lay the tagboard square on the floor and quickly paint its entire surface with a color of ink highly con-

LEFT: Splash Starbursts
RIGHT: Color Swirl

trasting with the ink in the medicine dropper. Before this ink has time to dry, hold the medicine dropper at about waist level and drop drops of ink onto the wet ink on the tagboard. (Drop about 5 to 7 drops.) You cannot accurately control the "landing spot" of each drop, but do your best to arrange them in an interesting pattern. The drops will splash and their color will spread outward into starburst patterns in the wet ink. Keep the paper flat until all ink dries.

33. COLOR SWIRLS (Shown on page 35, right)

A. Materials: Tagboard, white glue, colored drawing ink and brushes are needed for this activity. Cut the tagboard pieces quite small (the example shown is about 5 square inches, 12.5 square cm) as large designs would require immense quantities of glue.

B. Procedure: Brush white glue thickly over the entire sheet of tagboard, starting at the center and spiraling out toward the edges, or creating looped or waved designs with brush-stroke patterns in the glue. The object is to form ridged contour lines of glue. If the glue flattens and destroys brushed contour lines, simply wait several minutes for it to begin drying. As the glue begins to thicken, re-brush the contour patterns as previously described. Clean the brushes immediately (before glue dries and hardens) with warm, soapy water.

Allow the glue to dry thoroughly. (This may take overnight.) The opaque white glue changes to become glossy and transparent when dry, so you can tell by its color how the drying is progressing.

Brush a coat of colored drawing ink over the entire sheet, following the contour lines of the glue as you brush. The ink will not adhere evenly. High ridges of glue will remain uncolored and appear white, while ink collects in the low spots to accent the direction and contours of the design.

Some brands of ink and glue do not work as described. The ink does adhere evenly and solidly covers the entire sheet. In this case, let the ink dry. Then wipe over the surface with a damp paper towel or sponge. This will remove ink from the high ridges, exposing the white glue in those areas. Dark ink will remain in the hollows to accent the contour design.

34. GEOMETRIC RAINBOWS

A. Materials: Students will need lightweight tagboard, scissors, tempera paints, brushes and glue. A ruler and/or compass may be needed to draw the basic shapes.

B. Procedure: Cut two or three geometric shapes from tagboard, making them each a different shape and of graduated sizes. (These designs can be of any size desired. The largest shape could be 18 - 24 inches (45 - 61 cm) across for a gigantic, bold display. To conserve paper, they can be made smaller.) Paint each shape in bold stripes or swirls of color. Each shape should have a different pattern of colors.

When the paint is thoroughly dry, put the largest shape on the bottom, the medium shape on top of that and (if three shapes are used) the smallest shape on top. Each shape should be centered on the one below it. Glue the shapes in this position and allow the glue to dry thoroughly. Pin the completed design onto a sheet of colored paper for bulletin board display.

35. TISSUE REPEAT DESIGNS

A. Materials: Provide tissue paper, scissors, rubber cement and construction paper for mounting the completed designs.

B. Procedure: Use a sheet of tissue paper about 12 by 18 inches (30.5 by 45 cm). Fold the tissue paper in half lengthwise, then crosswise. Repeat until you have made five folds in all. With the paper still folded, cut away portions of tissue along each of the four sides. Be sure not to cut away an entire side — leave part of each folded edge uncut to hold the completed design together.

Open up the tissue to see the completed, lacey repeated design. Use a tiny spot of rubber cement at each corner to mount the tissue to a sheet of construction paper for display. The moisture in the cement tends to make the tissue paper warp and the colors bleed, so use as little cement as possible.

36. DIP AND DYE DESIGNS

A. Materials: White or pale-colored tissue paper and liquid food colors or colored drawing ink are needed for this activity.

B. Procedure: Fold a whole or half sheet of tissue paper into evenly spaced accordian pleats. With paper still folded, fold evenly spaced accordion pleats running in the opposite direction. The completed form will be a square of many thicknesses.

With paper folded, dip one corner into food coloring or colored ink. Hold it in the dye only long enough for color to absorb partway up into the tissue. The dye absorbs quickly, so be prepared to dip and remove the paper quickly. If dye color is too dark, add water to dilute the color. Dip each corner of the folded tissue into dye. (Each corner may be dipped in a different color if desired.)

An interesting effect can be obtained by dipping a single corner in two colors. First, dip it into a pale color allowing the dye to absorb high up into the tissue. Then, dip it quickly in and out of a darker color. The large, light-colored area will now have a dark center.

Open up the folds carefully (wet tissue tears easily) to see the colored design. Allow the dye to dry thoroughly, then pin the tissue to the bulletin board for display.

37. SILHOUETTES

A. Materials: Students will need black and white construction paper, pencil, scissors and glue. (You may need fine manicure scissors, a single-edged razor blade or pen knife for cutting fine details. If a razor blade or pen knife is used, place the paper on an old magazine or very thick pad of newspapers so the knife will not cut into the table top.)

B. Procedure: First, cut a very basic silhouette shape from black construction paper. Leaves, fish, faces, animals or flowers make good subjects for this project. Study the cut-out carefully. Decide what areas from within the shape could be cut away to create greater realism.

If you have cut a leaf silhouette, could paper be cut away to suggest the veining of the leaf? If it is an animal shape, could you cut away pieces to suggest facial features, fur, stripes or leg positions?

With pencil, lightly outline the areas you wish to cut away. Use manicure scissors, a razor blade or pen knife to cut away these areas. When the silhouette is complete, paste it onto a mounting sheet of white construction paper.

Example:

Basic Silhouette

Cut-Away Details
Added

SECTION II:
"The Third Dimension"

Projects in relief and free standing sculptures.

TOP ROW: String Snips, Salt Picture
BOTTOM ROW: Tissue Fluff, Spackled Collage

1. STRING SNIPS (Shown on page 43, upper left)

A. Materials: Provide construction paper or tagboard mounting sheets, scissors, white glue, scraps of yarn and string, rope, jute, etc., in a variety of thicknesses and colors.

B. Procedure: Cut string pieces of various lengths, thicknesses and colors. (Ends of string can be unbraided or combed to make fluffy fringe.) Lay the pieces on the mounting sheet to create an interesting pattern of line and color. Make many trial arrangements until the overall pattern pleases you. Then, lift one piece at a time, apply a few drops of glue here and there and press it back into place on the mounting sheet. Continue in this way gluing all pieces in place. Allow the work to stand undisturbed until the glue dries thoroughly.

2. SALT PICTURES (Shown on page 43, upper right)

A. Materials: Heavy cardboard, pencil, salt, flour, mixing bowls, spoon, water colors or tempera paints and brushes are needed for this activity. (Clear shellac is optional.)

B. Procedure: Make a modeling compound by mixing two parts salt with one part flour. Add cold water slowly, stirring to make a very thick, smooth paste.

On heavy cardboard, draw the outline of the design to be modeled. Spoon the modeling compound onto the cardboard, first following the penciled outlines, then filling in the center. Use your fingers to shape the mixture into relief designs. To speed drying time, make no areas over 1/2 inch thick with the modeling compound. Spread a very thin layer of the compound over all background areas to make a uniform surface for painting.

Allow the compound to dry slowly, out of direct heat or sunlight. (It may crack if it dries too quickly.) Drying time will be 2 - 5 days, depending on thickness of application, room temperature and humidity.

When the work is completely dry, the surface may be painted with water colors or tempera paint. (When the paint has dried, a light coat of clear shellac gives a nice final finish to the work.)

Handle these projects carefully. If the cardboard is bent or the construction is dropped, the salt compound will crack and/or loosen from the backing.

3. TISSUE FLUFFS (Shown on page 43, lower left)

A. Materials: Students will need tissue paper in a wide variety of colors, paper cutter and/or scissors, white glue, pencil and drawing paper.

B. Procedure: Cut tissue squares in many colors. (Use a paper cutter or scissors to cut tissue into strips one inch wide. Then cut the strips into one inch squares. Cut as many thicknesses as possible at once to save time. A committee of children may prepare these squares in advance of the art lesson if desired, sorting separate colors into separate boxes.)

Draw a realistic or abstract design on drawing paper. The design should be simple with no fine detail. Spread glue in one small area of the design. Crumple squares of tissue into loose wads and lay the wads side by side in the glued area to completely cover the backing paper. Continue in this way to cover the entire sheet, changing colors as needed to create the desired pattern. Keep the finished work flat until the glue dries thoroughly.

4. SPACKLED COLLAGE (Shown on page 43, lower right)

A. Materials: Old boards or pieces of extremely thick, sturdy cardboard, white glue, spackle (do NOT use Plaster of Paris — it dries much too quickly), disposable container in which to mix the spackle and metallic colored spray paint are needed for this activity. (Any color of paint could be used, if desired, and the color could be brushed rather than sprayed. Metallic colors are particularly effective, however, and spraying is the quickest, easiest method of applying the paint.)

You will also need a group of related objects to form the relief design. The example shown on page 43 was made from plastic and metal lids. You could use a group of broken, rusty tools (a screwdriver, pliers, nails, etc.) discarded kitchen utensils (wooden spoons, can openers, spatulas, etc.), a grouping of seashells, driftwood, a grouping of various sized empty spice cans, etc. All pieces used in the collage should be of a similar type, of interesting shape and relatively light in weight.

B. Procedure: Make many trial arrangements of the materials on the board. When you achieve a pleasing pattern, lift one object at a time, apply glue generously to the back surface and press it back onto the board in the desired position. Glue down all objects in this same way. Allow glue to dry thoroughly (several hours or overnight).

Mix spackle with cold water according to package directions. (It should be about the consistency of heavy cream.) Use a paint brush or your hands to spread the spackle evenly over all surfaces of the design pieces and background. Spread the spackle thinly — its purpose is simply to provide a unified appearance to the overall design and to make all surfaces accept paint equally well.

Wipe off your hands and/or brushes with paper towels, removing as much spackle as possible before washing in the sink. Allow unused spackle to harden in the disposable mixing containers, then discard with the trash. DO NOT POUR MIXTURE DOWN THE SINK. It will harden and clog the drains.

Allow the spackle to dry completely (overnight), then spray or brush with paint.

If a cardboard backing is used, do not bend the completed work or the spackle will crack and loosen from the backing.

5. RING RELIEF DESIGNS

A. Materials: Students will need construction paper in many colors, a paper cutter, cellophane tape and white glue.

B. Procedure: Cut colored construction paper into strips of various lengths. (Strips can be cut all one width or can vary from about 1/4 inch to 1 inch for depth variation.) Roll the strips into rings of various sizes. Fasten the rings with cellophane tape.

Lay the rings on a whole sheet of construction paper. Arrange them this way and that until they form a pleasing overall pattern. Then lift one ring at a time, put a few drops of glue on the cut edge and set the ring back in place on the paper. Press down a little on each ring to secure it firmly against the backing sheet. Let the work lie undisturbed until the glue dries thoroughly.

Example:

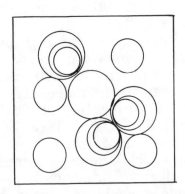

6. TOOTHPICK CONSTRUCTIONS

A. Materials: Provide dried peas (whole, not split), round toothpicks, a large bowl or pail and water.

B. Procedure: Place the peas in a large bowl or pail and completely cover them with cold water. The water should stand an inch or more over the top layer of peas. The extra water allows for absorption so the peas remain covered with water throughout the soaking period. Let the peas soak at least eight hours. Overnight is fine. Then, drain off the water.

The peas are now softened and can be used as connectors for toothpick constructions. Push toothpicks into the peas, joining as needed for the desired construction project. The entire project must be completed while the peas are damp and soft. As the peas dry, they shrink and harden, holding the toothpicks very firmly in place. The dried structure is amazingly sturdy.

Example:

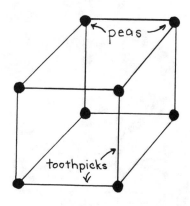

7. EGG CARTON MURAL (Shown on page 50)

A. Materials: Pressed paper egg cartons, scissors, tempera paints and brushes are needed for this activity.

B. Procedure: Cut the lids from pressed paper egg cartons. (This project uses only the bottom sections of the cartons.) Turn the bottom section of the carton upside down. Paint the entire surface with one color of tempera paint. Allow this paint to dry thoroughly.

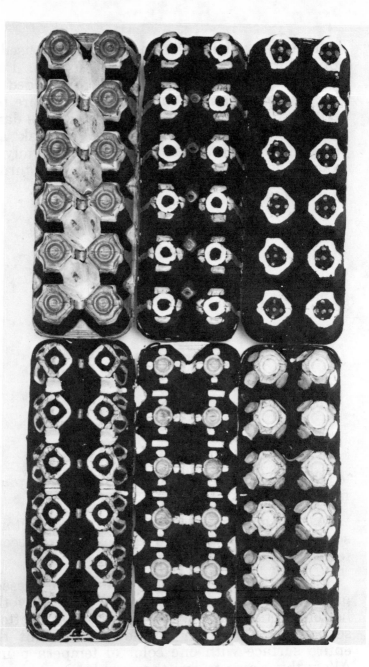

Egg Carton Mural

Use tempera paints in a variety of colors to decorate each cup of the carton in an abstract, geometric or realistic pattern. Each cup of the same carton should repeat the same design.

When this paint has dried, pin the cartons side by side on the bulletin board to create a giant three-dimensional mural.

In the mural shown on page 50, each separate carton was painted by a different child. Yet continuity of design was achieved by using all identically-shaped cartons, painting all cartons with the same background color (in this case black) and using the same colors for decorations. (In this case, all children used red, orange, yellow and white for the painted decorations.)

8. PINPRICK PICTURES

A. Materials: Students will need white paper, pencil, a straight pin and a pad of soft cloths. (A pad of newspapers or magazines WILL NOT WORK. The pad MUST be cloth.) A shallow container of water is also needed if Method 2 is used.

B. Procedure: The type of paper used effects the results of this project. Try Method 1 in a small area of the design. If it does not produce the described results, use Method 2.

Method 1: Use a pencil to draw the desired design on white drawing paper. Set the paper on a pad of soft cloths. Use a straight pin to puncture many evenly-spaced holes along the penciled guidelines on the paper.

After pricking several holes, turn the sheet over to look at the back side of the paper. This is the side to be displayed when the work is completed. The holes should appear very slightly raised, looking like miniature volcano cones with holes in the center. They will form slight shadows when displayed.

If you have achieved this effect, turn the paper back over to show the penciled design and continue pricking evenly spaced holes along every line of the pattern. When completed, display the picture with the raised side showing. If holes are flat, change to Method 2.

Method 2: Use your fingers to spread a small amount of water over a small section of the design. The paper should be only damp, not soggy. Prick evenly-spaced holes along each section of the design in this dampened area. Then dampen a new area and continue as directed to complete the design.

Example:

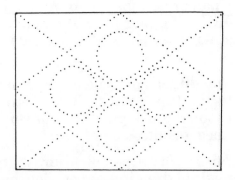

9. TISSUE CONSTRUCTIONS

A. Materials: Provide tissue paper in many colors, thin, pliable wire, wire cutters or pliers with a wire cutting edge, scissors and white glue. Felt pens may be used for decorations if desired.

B. Procedure: Bend wire into flat, two-dimensional shapes. Secure joints by wrapping wire ends together. Paint white glue along one edge of the wire. Lay the glued side of the wire onto tissue paper. When the glue has thoroughly dried, carefully trim away any tissue extending beyond the margins of the wire. Wire now follows closely along all outer margins of the tissue shape on the back side and is totally invisible from the front. Work in this way to complete each section of the construction. Then, fasten sections together as needed by wrapping joints with lengths of wire.

Decorate the tissue constructions as desired. Overlay pieces cut from other colors of tissue paper or draw on designs with felt pens.

A variety of display possibilities are illustrated below. Figure 1 shows separate pieces strung on thread to form a mobile. In figure 2, wire is wrapped to fasten onto a completed butterfly form, then stabbed into a cork display base. Figure 3 shows flowers displayed in a cardboard tube vase. Dotted lines indicate wire lying under the tissue surface of each construction.

Example:

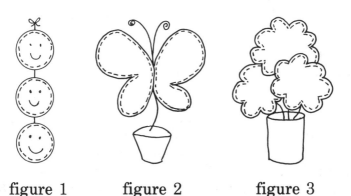

figure 1   figure 2   figure 3

—53—

10. MOLDED STYROFOAM MURAL

A. Materials: Bulletin board space, straight pins and blocks of white molded Styrofoam used in packaging fragile items for shipping are needed for this activity. The Styrofoam is formed to fit the exact shape of the object it protects, so each piece has a distinct personal "character."

Ask children to bring in pieces of molded Styrofoam. Or inquire at a store that handles electronic equipment — calculators, stereo equipment and the like often come packaged in this material and a clerk may be willing to save pieces for you. When the collection is large enough, this project can begin.

B. Procedure: Lay the molded Styrofoam pieces on the floor. Begin many trial arrangements, placing pieces closely side by side to create an artistically pleasing overall pattern.

When the design is satisfying, pin each piece to the bulletin board to duplicate the pattern arranged on the floor. If you have a large supply of Styrofoam, the mural can be big enough to cover an entire wall. Or, if a few pieces are available, the mural can be much smaller. The play of light and shadows on the contours of the white blocks adds interest to these designs.

11. MEDIEVAL CASTLE (Shown on page 55)

A. Materials: Students will need tagboard, masking tape, scissors, flour, salt, a mixing bowl, spatula, spoon, gray tempera paint, brushes and a cardboard box. (The basic portion of the castle is made from a cardboard box. The box can be as

Medieval Castle

small as a matchbox or as large as a giant refrigerator carton.)

B. Procedure: The cardboard box is the main castle section. Turn the box upside down so the solid bottom section becomes the castle roof. Cut windows and doors as desired. (Or, these features can be painted on later if preferred.)

Cut strips of tagboard to use as the parapet. Cut the strip the length of the box's perimeter and of whatever width suits the scale of the castle. Cut regularly spaced notched shapes from the top edge of this strip (see figure 1). Use masking tape to secure the strip to the top edges of the box allowing the notched design to extend up higher than the flat roof line (see figure 2).

Example:

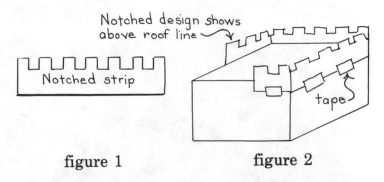

figure 1   figure 2

Castle towers can be made from pieces of tagboard rolled and taped to form cylinders. Or, use cardboard tubes from the centers of paper towel rolls or bathroom tissue if they are of appropriate size for the scale of the castle. The notched parapet design can be cut into the top edge of these cylinders or made from separate strips of tagboard taped in place just as was done on the main castle section. Glue or tape these towers to the castle positioning them as desired.

Mix equal quantities of flour and salt in a bowl. Slowly add cold water, stirring constantly, until the mixture has the consistency of very heavy cream. Use a spatula or your hands to spread this mixture thinly over the entire exterior of the castle, parapets and towers. (If the mixture is too runny to adhere, add more flour and salt. If it is too thick to spread easily, add more water.) The mixture should adhere easily and give the castle a granular, stone-like appearance. Allow this covering to dry thoroughly.

Mix enough light gray tempera paint in one batch to paint the entire exterior of the castle. (A second batch may not match the first exactly and give a blotchy appearance to the color. If you must finish with a second batch of paint, end one color and begin another at a corner where an imperfect color match is not as apparent.)

Other decorative features may be added as desired. In the castle photographed on page 55, a few brush strokes of black paint suggest stonework. The castle sits on a "grassy" Astroturf doormat.

A moat could be cut from aluminum foil and laid in place to surround the castle. Small tree branches set into the center holes of empty thread spools make realistic trees for scenery. Children may own plastic knights and horses they could bring in to add even more realism to the scene.

12. PAPER CLIP MOBILE

A. Materials: Provide paper clips and black thread for suspending the completed mobile.

B. Procedure: Swing the two loops of a paper clip past each other to create a small hanging loop at the top (see figure 1). Bend out the two arms. The clip is now shaped somewhat like the letter W (see figure 2). Make a quantity of these shapes.

Example:

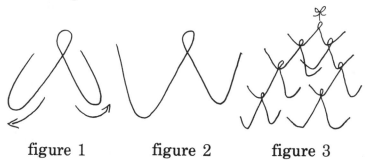

figure 1   figure 2   figure 3

Slip the center loop of one clip over the arm of another. Continue hanging clips in this way to create a mobile of the desired size (see figure 3).

Tie a length of black thread to the loop of the top clip of the mobile. Hang it where it is free to move and turn with the breeze. As it moves, the clips reflect light and appear to sparkle.

13. HARDWARE HEADS

A. **Materials:** Heavy cardboard, pencil and white glue are needed for this activity. You will also need an assortment of scrap hardware materials; such as, nuts, bolts, nails, clock parts, springs, chains and wire.

B. **Procedure:** With a pencil, lightly draw the outline of a head on the cardboard. Make facial features, hair, etc., by gluing scrap hardware pieces onto the outline. Large washers could be used for eyes, small nails for teeth, chains for hair and so on.

Try several arrangements of the scrap pieces until you are satisfied with the effect. Then, lift one piece at a time, apply glue to the back surface and set it back in place. Leave the finished work flat until the glue is thoroughly dry (several hours or overnight). Then, the "Hardware Heads" can be pinned to the bulletin board for display.

14. IN-THE-ROUND

A. **Materials:** Students will need a firm wire ring and decorative materials as described. The quickest way to make a wire ring is simply stretch out the bottom section of a wire coat hanger and form it into as perfect a circle as possible. Leave the hook portion of the hanger attached. Any other round frame such as an embroidery hoop could be used. If the frame is wrapped with yarn or string before being used, this wrapping will prevent tied-on pieces from slipping around the frame.

B. Procedure: "In-The-Round" designs are made by running strands of yarn, string, jute or fabric strips across the wire frame to create artistic patterns.

Four ideas are listed to serve as inspirations. Read them over, then let your creative imagination take over to think up other possibilities for artistic designs.

1. Run strips of patterned fabric across the frame in horizontal rows. Fold ends of the strips over the frame and staple or stitch them to hold the strips in place.

Run lengths of yarn or jute across the frame in open spaces between the cloth strips. String beads on the yarn. (Beads can be hand made of self-hardening clay.)

2. Tie lengths of yarn or jute across the frame to create an abstract line design. Use all one color yarn, or combine two or more colors. Beads can be placed here and there along the strands if desired. Place a dot of white glue on knots where yarn is tied to the frame. This keeps knots from untying and also keeps the knot from slipping around the frame.

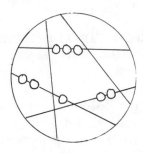

3. Tie lengths of yarn or jute across the frame to create an abstract line design as described in #2. Tie warp threads across some areas, then weave in and out of these warp threads to fill some areas with woven designs.

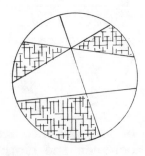

4. Tie a string across the top portion of the wire loop. Suspend decorative beads, feathers, shells, etc., from this string. Tie closely spaced rows of string across the bottom section of the wire loop. Weave in and out of these strings to create a woven design in that portion of the loop.

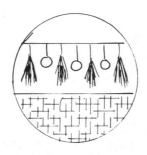

15. CORREGATED STRIP CREATIONS
(Shown on page 62, top row)

A. Materials: Provide corregated cardboard with corregation ridges exposed, smooth-surfaced cardboard, paper cutter and/or scissors, ruler, pencil, white glue in a squeeze-top bottle and straight pins.

B. Procedure: Cut the smooth-surfaced cardboard into the desired size for a mounting sheet. Cut the ridged, corregated cardboard into strips about 3/4 inch wide. (A sharp paper cutter speeds this process.) On the smooth-surfaced cardboard, sketch the design to be created.

The photograph on page 62 shows a caricature type profile and a formal geometric design to indicate the wide range of design possibilities.

Squeeze a thick line of glue along one penciled guideline. Set a strip of corregated cardboard on edge into the glue. Press down on the strip so it is well imbedded in the glue. Continue in this way to create the sketched design with upright corregated strips. (The corregated cardboard strip has a wide, stable edge and will stand up with little or no help. If it does slip out of position, push a straight pin at an angle through the

TOP ROW: Corregated Strip Creations (2 examples)
BOTTOM ROW: Corregated Cut-Outs, Corregated Dizzies

bottom half of the strip and into the cardboard mounting sheet to hold the pieces together while the glue dries. Curved strips sometimes require more pinning to hold them in position while the glue dries.) Leave the completed work flat until the glue dries thoroughly.

16. CORREGATED CUTOUTS (Shown on page 62, lower left)

A. Materials: Corregated cardboard with corregation ridges exposed, scissors, pencil, white glue and heavy smooth-surfaced cardboard on which to mount the completed designs are needed for this activity.

B. Procedure: Use a pencil to draw one or more shapes on a sheet of corregated cardboard. (Shapes should be simple with no fine detail.) Cut these shapes out of the cardboard, then glue the background piece (the sheet with cut-out holes) onto heavy, smooth cardboard. Use the pieces you have just cut as patterns for the next step of this project. Trace the cut shapes on another piece of corregated cardboard, making sure the ridges of corregation run in the opposite direction they do on the pattern pieces. Cut out these new shapes then fit and glue them into the holes from which the first shapes were cut. The corregation lines in the background and design pieces now run in opposite directions.

Younger children may have difficulty tracing and cutting accurately enough for the new pieces to fit snugly into the cut holes.

C. Variation: Here is another way to achieve almost the same effect. Glue a solid, uncut sheet of corregated cardboard onto a mounting sheet to hold it flat. From another sheet of corregated cardboard, cut shapes with corregation lines running in the opposite direction as the background. Glue these cut out pieces on top of the uncut background sheet. Lay a book over the completed work to hold the cut pieces firmly against the background while the glue dries.

17. CORREGATED DIZZIES (Shown on page 62, lower right)

A. **Materials:** Students will need corregated cardboard with corregation ridges exposed, tempera paint, brushes, round shapes for tracing circles (use tin cans, spools, cups, etc.), pencil, scissors, white glue and heavy, smooth surfaced cardboard.

B. **Procedure:** Paint a sheet of ridged, corregated cardboard in a free-form pattern of two colors. The example on page 62 is done in black and white. A combination of optically vibrating colors (see "The Use Of Color In Op Art," page 213) will produce an even greater dizzying effect.

When the paint is thoroughly dry, trace circle shapes onto this sheet. Each circle should overlap areas of two colors. Carefully cut out the circles. Glue the background piece (the sheet from which you just cut the circles) onto a mounting sheet of heavy, smooth cardboard. This will hold the work flat. Glue each cutout circle back into the hole from which it was cut, but turn it so both the direction of the corregation lines and the pattern of colors are out of alignment from their original positions. Step back and take a look. Can you see why these are called "Dizzies?"

UPPER LEFT: All Of A Kind (2 examples)
UPPER RIGHT: Plastic Bubble Art
LOWER LEFT: Faces In A Crowd
LOWER RIGHT: Siamese Cat

18. ALL OF A KIND (Shown on page 65, upper and center left)

A. Materials: Provide tagboard mounting sheets, white glue and a quantity of identical objects. The objects may be toothpicks, dried beans, cotton swabs, macaroni, paper clips, gummed paper reinforcements, etc.

B. Procedure: The object of this project is to take a quantity of identical objects and arrange them to form a picture or design. It is a test of your imagination and creativity!

Put a number of the objects on the mounting sheet. Arrange the objects until some pattern takes form in your mind. Then, begin gluing the objects in place as needed.

The photograph on page 65 shows toothpicks arranged in vertical and horizontal blocks to form an overall pattern. The other example shows salad macaroni used to make a butterfly. Some of the pieces are laid on their sides, others stand upright so you can see into the tubes. This variation in position of the pieces adds texture interest to the design.

19. PLASTIC BUBBLE ART (Shown on page 65, upper right)

A. Materials: Pieces of bubble plastic are needed for this activity. (This is used for cushioning fragile items for shipping and consists of two laminated sheets of clear plastic film with air bubbles trapped between the layers. The bubbles are placed in regular geometric alignment.) Enamel paints (other types of paint will NOT adhere to plastic), brushes and solvent for cleaning the brushes are also needed. Very little paint is used in this project. A few of the small bottles used for painting children's models will probably be enough for the entire class.

SAFETY PRECAUTION: Make sure the room is well ventilated while working with enamel paints and/or solvent.

B. Procedure: Look at the pattern of bubbles in the plastic. They are arranged in definite diagonal and vertical rows. Study it carefully, then use enamel colors to paint the tops of the bubbles to accentuate a pattern you see. The plastic surface of each bubble is "squishy" — it moves around as you try to paint it. Have quite a bit of paint on the brush, set the brush on the bubble top and use a scrubbing motion to paint a circle shape. The circles will not be perfectly round, but they will give a round appearance when the work is done. Change colors as needed to produce the desired design. Clean the paintbrushes with solvent as soon as painting is completed.

When the paint has thoroughly dried (it dries very quickly), the work can be stapled or pinned to a sheet of construction paper for bulletin board display. The construction paper color will show through the clear areas of the plastic, so choose a color that goes well with those in the design.

20. FACES IN A CROWD (Shown on page 65, lower left)

A. Materials: Provide cardboard tubes (centers from rolls of paper towels, bathroom tissue, etc.) in several sizes, black tempera paint, brushes and paper clips. Decorative features may be painted with tempera paint, cut from colored construction paper and glued in place, etc. Yarn, string, fabric scraps, etc., can be used for decorative features as desired.

B. Procedure: Paint several cardboard tubes of various heights and diameters with black tempera paint. Allow the paint to dry thoroughly.

Each tube will become one "person" in the arrangement. Add decorative features as desired to make faces, hair, clothing details, etc.

Arrange the tubes to stand side by side touching each other to form a crowd-like grouping. Use paper clips to fasten the tubes together. Clip the bottom edge of two tubes together. Continue clipping additional tubes to those already fastened.

21. SIAMESE CATS (Shown on page 65, lower right)

A. Materials: For each cat you will need one slender pop bottle (the example shown in the photograph on page 65 was made from a 7-ounce 7-UP bottle), a burned out 15 - 25 watt lightbulb, masking tape and spray paint. Decorative features may be cut from paper or fabric scraps and glued in place.

B. Procedure: Set the lightbulb on the mouth of the bottle. (The bulb will not fit into the bottle but simply rests on top.) Hold the bulb in place and wrap the joint of the bulb and bottle with masking tape to hold the bulb securely in place. This construction forms the cat's head and body.

Spread a protective layer of old newspapers on the floor and spray the bottle construction with paint. Several thin coats of paint give better coverage than one thick coat. Allow each coat of paint to dry thoroughly before applying the next.

Cut decorative features (eyes, feet, tail, collar, etc.) from paper or cloth scraps. Glue them onto the cat's body to complete the figure.

Various color combinations give the cats totally different "personalities." (The cat shown on page 65 is black and white.) If the bottle and bulb are sprayed metallic silver and the decorative features are cut from black felt, the cat assumes a regal, elegant character. Spraying the bottle and bulb beige and cutting the features from dark brown fake fur scraps produces genuine Siamese cat coloration. Or, for a zany variation, spray the bottle and bulb hot pink. Cut the decorations from bright red felt. Glue a few fake "jewels" to the collar. Let your imagination be your guide.

22. SURREALISTIC ARRANGEMENTS
(Shown on page 70)

A. Materials: Each arrangement is different and uses totally different materials. Use common household items or construct the needed parts out of any suitable materials.

B. Procedure: The surrealistic arrangement, like the surrealistic collage (see page 15) combines totally normal, realistic objects to create a scene that is absurd, surprising or downright shocking.

For best understanding of this concept, study the examples shown on page 70. Do you ever feel you are "going under" with homework? The rubber hand and book arrangement is a silly illustration of this feeling.

Surrealistic Arrangements

A sardine can holds a host of identical, stark, construction paper people. At first glance silly, on second thought perhaps a statement about our industrialized society.

A glass jar is lined with cut paper faces. It looks as if the jar is stuffed full of people. A laughing doll sits amidst the coils of a hideous rubber snake. Large lensed sunglasses have built-in eyes.

These arrangements take highly creative thought and careful planning. Not all children may be able to handle this task, so it is best handled as a voluntary, free-time assignment. Explain the concept, display the above photograph and let the children work on ideas in their free time or at home. Provide a display table where children may place their completed arrangements.

Repeatedly stress the "rules" for surrealism: the arrangement should create a scene that is absurd, surprising or downright shocking.

23. BREAD DOUGH SCULPTURE

A. Materials: Students will need bread dough (recipe follows), aluminum foil, flat cookie sheets and a baking oven. Scissors or sharp knives may be used for slashing and cutting the dough. Paint is optional.

BREAD DOUGH RECIPE

1 package dry yeast
2 cups warm water
3 tablespoons sugar
} Mix together to dissolve yeast, let stand five minutes for yeast to begin working.

2 tablespoons salt
1/4 cup cooking oil
7 cups flour
} Add

Stir until thoroughly mixed. Knead until dough is smooth and elastic. Cover and let rise until double in bulk (about one hour or more, depending on room temperature). Punch down the dough and it is ready for use in "Bread Dough Sculptures."

B. Procedure: Wash your hands very thoroughly with soap and water. Break off pieces of bread dough and use it just like clay to form a sculpture. Animals, birds or flowers make good subjects for this art. The dough can be cut with scissors or knives to form shapes or to make slashed designs on those shapes. Additional pieces can be set on top or close beside the original piece. They will join together as the dough rises. Keep the sculpture flat. You cannot build tall structures with this medium.

As you complete the shapes, set them on a foil covered cookie sheet, cover them with a clean cloth and allow the dough to rise until nearly double in bulk. This will take 45 minutes to an hour depending on room temperature.

Bake the sculptures in an oven preheated to 400° for 12 - 20 minutes, or until lightly browned. Small pieces will finish baking sooner and can be removed from the oven before large pieces are done.

If desired, the sculptures can be painted with food coloring thinned with water to produce pale colors. Use CLEAN water color brushes to brush on the color.

There is an added bonus to this project. The sculptures are deliciously edible!

SECTION III:

"South Of The Border"

Projects inspired by traditional Mexican, Central and South American folk arts, with materials and working methods adapted for easy classroom use.

UPPER LEFT: Tree Of Life
UPPER RIGHT: Black Work
CENTER: Piñata
LOWER LEFT: Yarn Painting (2 examples)
LOWER RIGHT: Amatl Painting

1. TREE OF LIFE (Shown on page 75, upper left)

A. Materials: Provide construction paper in many bright colors, mounting sheets, scissors and glue.

B. Procedure: In Latin American countries, the "Tree Of Life" is a traditional decoration usually made as a free-standing sculpture from clay or papier mâche decorated with bright colored paints. You can make the same kind of design with colored paper.

First, cut a branched tree shape from construction paper and glue it onto a mounting sheet. Cut shapes of leaves, birds, flowers, animals, etc., from construction paper and glue them onto the branches. Use cut paper shapes glued onto these figures for additional decorations.

2. BLACK WORK (Shown on page 75, upper right)

A. Materials: Students will need burlap or linen-textured fabric in off-white or tan, pencil, black yarn or embroidery floss, yarn or embroidery needles. Provide books with illustrations of typical South American art designs.

B. Procedure: Look through these books showing typical South American art designs. You can use these as an inspiration for your own design creation. The design should be a simple line drawing, primitive in appearance.

With a pencil, draw the design on fabric. Use black yarn or black embroidery floss to embroider the outline of the design. When the embroidery is done, pull threads along each margin of the fabric to make a fringed border.

3. PIÑATA (Shown on page 75, center)

A. Materials: Scissors and tissue paper in several colors are needed for each Piñata type described. While any adhesive may be used, rubber cement causes the least color-run and warping of the tissue paper. Other materials are listed with each specific type of Piñata.

B. Procedure:

1. Round Piñata: (This Piñata is breakable and can be used for the Piñata game described in Part C.) Blow up a balloon. Mark a 3-inch square on the balloon indicating where the opening will be for inserting candies.

Mix flour and water paste in a disposable container (the paste should be the consistency of heavy cream). Cut or tear old newspapers into strips about 1 - 2 inches wide. Dip a strip of newspaper into the paste, then run it between your thumb and forefinger to remove any excess paste. Apply the strip to the balloon, making sure not to cover the marked opening. Cover the entire balloon (except the opening) with pasted strips. Apply about four layers of pasted strips to the balloon. To keep track of layers, make one layer black and white strips, the next of strips cut from colored comics, or apply one layer lengthwise and the next crosswise.

Allow the form to dry completely. This will take 1 - 2 days. Wrap string in several directions around the form to make a hanging sling. Leave a length of string at the top for hanging. Press a pin through the Piñata opening to puncture the balloon inside.

Cut colored tissue paper strips about 3 inches wide. (To speed the cutting process, leave the tissue folded just as it came in the package. Use a paper cutter to cut through all thicknesses at 3-inch intervals.) Fold one strip in half lengthwise. Along the folded edge, make cuts about 1-inch deep with about 8 cuts per inch (see figure 1). Turn the strip inside out. The sharp folded crease is now inside, pointed downward, with a rounded hump on each side (see figure 2). Paste the bottom edges together.

Example:

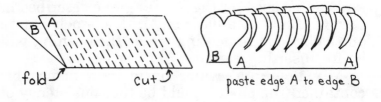

figure 1

figure 2
Paste edge A
to edge B

(After children understand this cutting procedure, they can stack 6 - 8 strips on top of each other, then fold and cut all these strips as a single unit to save time. The strips must be separated and individually turned inside out and pasted.)

Begin cementing these ruffled tissue strips to the Piñata form in even rows. Each ruffled row should cover the pasted edge of the previous strip. Do not cover the opening left for inserting candies.

Example:

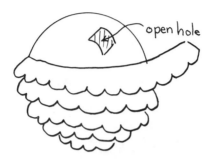

Cutting and applying the ruffles takes time. Children who do not finish the project during art class could continue working on it during free time.

2. Box Piñata: (This Piñata is decorative only. It is too sturdy to break in the Piñata game as described in Part C.) You will need a box (shoe box, oatmeal box — any shape), tape and string in addition to the materials listed in Part A.

Tape the box lid securely onto the box. Make a string sling to hold the Piñata. Simply tie string in two directions around the box, leaving a length at the top for suspending the Piñata.

Cover the shape with tissue paper ruffles as described in the directions for the Round Piñata.

3. Star-Shaped Piñata: (This Piñata is decorative only. It is too sturdy to break in the Piñata game as described in Part C.) Use a square box as the basic form. Roll 6 cone shapes from lightweight tagboard. Securely tape one cone to each of the six sides of the box.

Example:

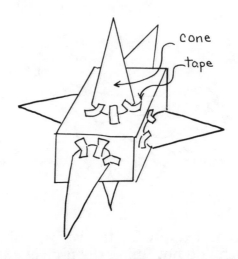

Tie a string sling around the form, then cover it with tissue ruffles as described in directions for the Round Piñata.

C. The Piñata Game: Throughout Latin America, the Piñata is used for any festive occasion. Place many small candies in the Piñata, then hang it from a rope strung between two trees (or whatever is convenient). It should be hung high above the heads of the children.

Blindfold one child and give him a long stick. Then, he tries to break the Piñata with the stick. While he is hitting, the Piñata can be slid to a new position along the rope to make it more difficult for him to find it and break it. Children watching must stand at a safe distance so they are not hit by the stick. Each child in turn is blindfolded and takes a turn trying to break the Piñata. When it is finally broken, candy spills onto the ground and all the children scramble to collect the goodies.

4. YARN PAINTING (2 examples shown on page 75, lower left)

A. Materials: Provide cardboard or tag-board, pencil, glue, cuticle stick and yarn scraps in many bright colors.

B. Procedure: In Mexico, yarn painting is done by spreading warm wax on a board and then pressing rows of colored yarn into the wax to produce the desired design.

Here is an easier way to produce the same effect. Use a pencil to draw a simple, silhouette-type shape on tagboard. Birds, flowers or animals make good designs. Spread glue around the outer margins of the tagboard. Lay three rows of yarn around the border. By tradition, each of these three border rows is of a different color. Turn sharp corners using a cuticle stick, or any other similar tool, to keep corners at sharp right angles and to press rows of yarn firmly against each other.

Spread glue along the penciled shape outline and lay a strand of yarn to form its border. Keep sharp corners on initial pattern outline rows. These sharp angles will gradually soften as work continues toward the center. Spread glue and lay in rows of yarn to fill in the center of this shape, again using the cuticle stick to push rows together and to push yarn into hard to reach corners. Change colors as needed for your pattern. Tuck loose ends under to hide them. Fill in the background in this same way, completing one section at a time.

5. AMATL PAINTINGS (Shown on page 75, lower right)

A. Materials: Amatl (ah MAH tel) is paper made of wet bark pounded flat. Several layers are pressed together, then dried.

As a substitute, use old grocery bags, the more used-looking the better. This resembles the color and texture of amatl paper. You will also need scissors, pencil, tempera paints and brushes or felt pens in a variety of colors.

B. Procedure: Cut long, rectangular shapes from paper bags. (This is the traditional shape for Amatl Paintings. Other shapes can be used if desired.) Use a pencil to sketch the design. Traditional designs are twining vine-type branches with leaves. Sitting among the branches are birds, animals and/or flowers. Use brilliant colors of tempera paint or felt pens to color the design: hot pink, bright orange, chartruese, electric blue, etc. These paintings should explode with color.

6. PERUVIAN TIN MASKS - TYPE I (Shown on page 83, upper right)

A. Materials: Scissors, cardboard, pencil, heavy string, white glue, common household aluminum foil and tape are needed for this activity.

B. Procedure: Use a pencil to draw a mask shape on cardboard. Cut out the shape. Then use a pencil to draw desired facial features on the mask. Spread on the glue and lay thick string along each penciled line. Allow the glue to dry thoroughly.

UPPER RIGHT: Peruvian Tin Mask, Type I
RIGHT: Giant Paper Flowers
CENTER LEFT: Columbian "Gold" Jewelry
LOWER LEFT: Mock Mola

Cut a sheet of aluminum foil larger than the cardboard mask. Lay the foil on top of the mask turning the extra margin under and pressing it flat against the back of the cardboard. If necessary, tape the overlapping foil to the back of the mask to hold it securely. Use your fingers to gently smooth the foil across the front of the mask, pressing it down so the string design stands out in raised relief.

7. PERUVIAN TIN MASKS - TYPE II

A. Materials: Students will need tin foil sold in sheets at craft supply stores, old newspapers, scissors, a ball point pen and a cuticle stick or similar tool for pressing designs.

B. Procedure: Make a thick pad of newspapers and lay the foil face down on this pad. Use a pencil to lightly sketch the desired facial design on the back of the tin sheet.

Use a ball point pen or cuticle stick to press down into the tin, drawing along penciled guidelines. Turn the tin over from time to time to check your progress. The grooved line dented into the back surface of the tin should appear as a line in raised relief on the front. Mistakes cannot be corrected, so work slowly and carefully.

When the design is complete, edges of the foil can be cut, fringed, curled, bent, etc., as needed to form hair, ears, etc.

8. GIANT PAPER FLOWERS (Shown on page 83, right)

A. Materials: Provide tissue paper, scissors, cellophane tape, straight pins, stiff wire and florist's tape.

B. Procedure: Cut three to seven circles of graduated size from tissue paper. The largest should be about 8 inches in diameter. The edges of these circles can be cut into scalloped shapes, slashed towards the center to produce a fringed effect or left plain.

Put a small square of cellophane tape in the center of each circle. This adds strength so the tissue will not tear during construction. Place the circles one on top of another with the largest on the bottom, then in graduated size with the smallest on top. Push a straight pin through the center of all layers (see figure 1). Holding the pin shaft in one hand, use the other hand to gently push the petals up around the pin head (see figure 2).

Lay the pin shaft against a length of stiff wire cut to the desired stem length. Wrap florist's tape around the base of the flower, the pin and the wire to secure all pieces firmly together (see figure 3). Continue wrapping downward to cover the entire length of wire.

Example:

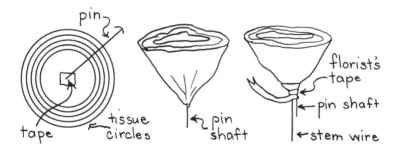

figure 1   figure 2   figure 3

In the photograph on page 83, the flowers are shown in a cardboard tube "vase."

9. COLUMBIAN "GOLD" JEWELRY
(Shown on page 83, left center)

A. Materials: Cardboard or tagboard, cotton parcel post cord, white glue, scissors, old newspapers, metallic gold paint, brushes and paint solvent for cleaning brushes are needed for this activity.

B. Procedure: With these simple materials you can duplicate Columbian jewelry designs made by soldering gold wire onto flat gold shapes.

Use scissors to cut a shape from cardboard. It should be an appropriate size and shape for a pendant or brooch. Cut lengths of cotton cord and make trial patterns of cord for the jewelry design. You may wish to form a traditional South American design or do something very modern.

When you have planned a pattern you like, spread glue on the shape and lay on the cord in the desired design. When the glue is thoroughly dry, spread old newspapers to protect the work surface, then paint the jewelry with gold or any other metallic-colored paint. Clean the brushes as soon as painting is completed.

10. MOCK MOLAS (Shown on page 83, lower left)

A. Materials: Provide construction paper or felt fabric in three colors, pencil, scissors and glue.

B. Procedure: In Central America, molas are made with many layers of fabric, each a different color. Designs are cut from each layer and the cut edges are carefully rolled and hemmed by hand. Then the pieces of fabric are stacked one on top of another with colors from each layer showing in the completed design. The layers are stitched together by hand. It is an intricate and time-consuming process.

Here is an easy way to create the same effect. Take three sheets of construction paper (or felt), each a different color. On one sheet, draw a silhouette-type shape and cut it out. Lay the border section of this sheet on the next sheet and trace the silhouette shape. Do not cut the shape from the second sheet. Using the traced outline to guide your pattern, draw decorative shapes within the outline. Cut away only these decorative shapes. Put the uncut sheet on the bottom, the sheet with decorative cut-outs on top of it and the sheet with the silhouette cut-out on the very top. See how all three colors show through in the finished design? Glue these three sheets together, stacked as previously described.

11. OJO DE DIOS (EYE OF GOD)
(Shown on page 90, upper right)

A. Materials: Students will need two lengths of dowel rods, two straight sticks, or two lengths cut from coathanger wire and yarn in two or more colors.

B. Procedure: Lay the two dowel rods crossing at right angles to each other (see figure 1). Wrap yarn several times around this joint to secure it firmly (see figure 2).

Example:

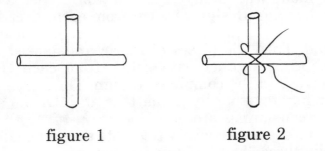

figure 1   figure 2

Carry yarn from spoke to spoke in sequence around the frame, tying on new colors as needed to create the desired pattern. Wrap yarn once around each spoke as you come to it.

Wrapping the yarn over the spoke, then under and back over heading towards the next spoke produces work totally covering the spokes from view (see figure 3). Wrapping yarn under, then over and under heading towards the next spoke produces work lying under the spokes, with wrapped spokes exposed (see figure 4). Wrapping twice (or more times) around each spoke as you come to it produces wider spacing between rows of yarn (see figure 5). Try all three methods for pattern variations.

Example:

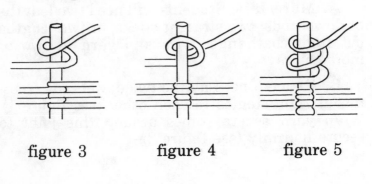

figure 3   figure 4   figure 5

When the design is complete, wrap any exposed lengths of spoke-ends with yarn. Tuck under the loose end of yarn and apply a drop of glue to hold it in place.

Decorative tassels may be added to the ends of spokes. Lay several strands of yarn over the spoke-end (see figure 6). Use another length of yarn to tie the strands tightly against the spoke (see figure 7).

Example:

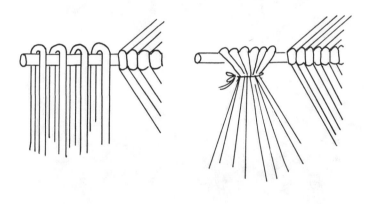

figure 6   figure 7

To make the larger, more complex design shown in the photograph on page 90, additional crossbars were added at the ends of the main pattern spokes. Each of these small designs was worked in the same way previously described. Lengths of sticks were used for the framework, so the frame is not as straight as if dowels had been used.

UPPER LEFT: Yarn Wrapped Sculptures
UPPER RIGHT: Ojo de Dios (Eye Of God)
LOWER LEFT: Feather Picture
LOWER RIGHT: Imitation Stone Carving

12. YARN WRAPPED SCULPTURES
(Shown on page 90, upper left)

A. Materials: Clay (or smooth stones), white glue, cuticle stick or any similar pointed tool and yarn scraps in many colors are needed for this activity.

B. Procedure: Use self-hardening clay to model a simple bird or animal form. Keep the model smooth and compact with no sharp angles or tiny appendages. Allow the clay to dry thoroughly. (If preferred, smooth stones can be used as the core for these sculptures.)

Spread one area of the clay figure with glue and cover the area with rows of yarn. (The yarn can be laid in straight rows, concentric circles, or in whatever pattern best fits the contours of the sculpture.) Use a cuticle stick to press rows together and to press yarn into hard-to-reach areas. Change colors as needed for the desired pattern. Continue in this way until the entire sculpture is covered with yarn.

13. IMITATION STONE CARVING (Shown on page 90, lower right)

A. Materials: Provide lightweight tagboard or shirt cardboard, scissors, white glue, tempera paints in gray or tan (or any other stone color) and paintbrushes. Gray or tan sand is optional.

You may wish to display pictures of early Panamanian stone carvings, pre-Columbian sculptures, etc., to give children an idea of the distinctive character and "flavor" of primitive carvings.

B. Procedure: Cut a basic silhouette-type shape from light cardboard. Cut decorative features from cardboard and glue them onto the basic shapes to form the desired figure in raised relief. In the finished design, the cardboard will be one layer thick in some areas, two or more layers thick in others. Weight down the finished work with a heavy book to keep pieces flat while the glue dries.

When the glue has thoroughly dried, paint the figures with thinly mixed stone-colored tempera paint. If the paint is too thick, it will hide the crisp ridge lines and destroy the relief effect. A very light touch of matching sand sprinkled into the wet paint heightens the stone effect.

14. FEATHER PICTURES (Shown on page 90, lower left)

A. Materials: Students will need feathers in several colors and sizes, pencil, glue and paper to be used as mounting sheets. Small, naturally colored feathers like those used in the example shown on page 90 can be purchased inexpensively in craft supply stores. Large, exotic and/or artificially colored feathers are more expensive.

B. Procedure: Feather painting is now a lost art in Mexico. Originally, tiny feathers were stripped to leave only a few "hairs" at the very tip. These tiny tips were glued in place, taking hours to produce a line of color that could have been painted with a single brush stroke. The finished work looked like a painting. You had to touch it to believe it had been made of feathers.

Craftsmen, still doing feather work now, use large feathers and the work is instantly recognized as being made of feathers. Today, we will make this kind of picture.

Use a pencil to sketch the desired design on paper. Pictures of flowers or birds work very well. Put glue on feathers of various colors and sizes and set them in place to create the desired pattern.

Most feather shafts have a stiff, natural curve. It is virtually impossible to glue them totally flat against the paper. Place a blob of glue on the thick end of the shaft and a small smear of glue on the feather tip. Press these ends against the paper. The center section of the feather will curve up from the paper, but the two glued ends will hold it in place. Allow the completed work to lie flat and undisturbed until the glue has dried thoroughly.

15. CUT TISSUE DECORATIONS (Shown at the top of page 94)

A. Materials: Tissue paper, pencils and scissors are needed for this activity.

B. Procedure: In Mexico, these tissue designs are strung up all over town on fiesta days.

Fold a piece of tissue paper in half. Draw half the desired design on the tissue with the design

Example:

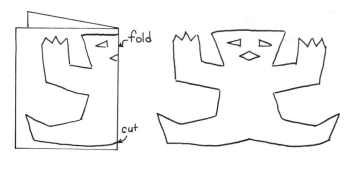

TOP: Cut Tissue Decorations
BOTTOM: Sun Face

center on the fold line. Figures should have a simple, primitive appearance. Cut the shape, open the paper and the design is made.

16. SUN FACES (Shown at the bottom of page 94)

A. Materials: Provide self-hardening clay, rolling pin, table knife, cuticle stick or other tool of similar shape, old newspapers and water. For a mold, use a small plate or saucer turned upside down to form a slightly dome-shaped curve. Use oilcloth turned shiny-side down or a bread board covered with old cotton sheeting for an excellent non-stick surface on which to roll the clay.

B. Procedure: Spread old newspapers on the work surface to protect it from clay smears. Use a rolling pin to roll clay into a slab about 3/8 inch thick. Roll in two directions so the slab is of uniform thickness throughout. Lay the plate face down on the clay. Cut a circle about 1/2 inch beyond the rim of the plate.

Cover the inverted plate with a single layer of newspaper. This keeps the clay from sticking to it. Lay the circle of clay onto the inverted plate and press it down to fit the contours of the plate. Trim away excess clay along the edges.

To form the sun's rays, cut narrow triangles from the clay slab. Mark the area where the ray and face will join. Score and slip these areas (see page 159 for "Score and Slip" directions). Press the triangles firmly in place. Reinforce each joint as described on page 159. Even placement of rays can be accomplished by thinking of the sun face as a clock face. First, put on rays at 12, 3, 6 and 9 o'clock. Then, add rays between these as needed.

Bend the end of each ray upward. Give the tip of each ray a slight clockwise twist. You may need to put small wads of crumpled paper under each ray to support its raised position while the clay dries.

Puncture two hanging holes near the rim of the face at positions of about 11 and 1 o'clock.

Roll slender ropes of clay about 1/8 inch thick. Cut needed lengths and lay them on the circle to form facial features as desired. Lay tiny bits of clay in the "cracks" between these clay ropes and the main body of clay. Use your water-dampened finger tips, a cuticle stick or damp cotton swab to smooth out all joints.

The eye pupils are made of tiny balls of clay set in place, then stabbed in the centers with a sharp pencil point. The stabbing fastens the pupils in place and produces the eye center.

When clay is leather-hard (still damp, but firm enough to hold its shape), remove it from the plate mold. When the clay is thoroughly dry, it can be painted with an earth-tone tempera paint. Immediately wipe the surface with a damp paper towel to remove paint from smooth, raised surfaces. Dark paint will remain in the grooves and hollows to highlight the design against the lighter background. The sun face pictured on page 94 was not stained in this way, but simply left in its natural clay color.

17. TIN LANTERNS

A. Materials: Students will need tin cans, brown wrapping paper, tape, pencil, hammer, nails and votive candles. You will also need freezer space.

B. Procedure: Remove top lids from tin cans of any size. Remove the paper labels, then thoroughly wash and dry the cans.

Cut brown wrapping paper in a strip the height of the can. Cut it long enough to wrap around the can with extra length for overlap. Mark the overlapping area so it will not be included in the design. Lay the paper flat on the table and draw the lines to form design patterns for the lantern. (These can be geometric designs or simple, realistic shapes.)

Fill the can with water and place it in a freezer. Small cans will take about 24 hours to freeze solidly while larger cans may take two full days, so begin this preparation well in advance. (If your school has no freezer, children can freeze the cans of water at home and bring them back on the designated work day.) After removing the cans from the freezer, have them begin work immediately so the ice blocks do not have time to melt.

Tape the paper pattern around the can. Lay the ice-filled can on its side. Use a hammer and nails to punch holes through the can along the guidelines of the paper pattern. Use nails of several sizes to produce large and small holes in the tin which adds interest to the design.

Pour out the ice, remove the paper pattern and allow the can to dry thoroughly. Set a small, votive candle in the lantern.

Example:

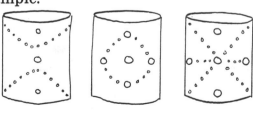

18. POTTERY

A. Materials: Cylindrical, square or rectangular pots made of self-hardening clay according to directions on pages 166 and 168, a cuticle stick or similarly pointed tool, tempera paint, brushes and paper towels or a sponge are needed for this activity. You may wish to display books showing pre-Columbian, Inca and/or Mayan art as design inspirations.

B. Procedure: When pots are completed and the clay has dried to a leather-hard stage (firm enough to hold its shape but still damp enough to be carved), use a cuticle stick, nail or other pointed tool to carve traditional Latin American designs in the clay.

When the clay is thoroughly dry, paint the entire surface with a dark colored tempera paint. Use damp paper towels or a sponge to wipe away the paint immediately. The flat surfaces of the clay will retain only faint color while the indented, carved designs will remain deeply colored to boldy emphasize the pattern.

19. WOVEN STRAW STARBURSTS

A. Materials: Provide stalks of straw or firm but pliable weed stems, scissors, thread and white glue.

B. Procedure: Lay four straws to form a star pattern. Tie thread around the center crossing joint to hold the pieces in this arrangement (see figure 1).

Example:

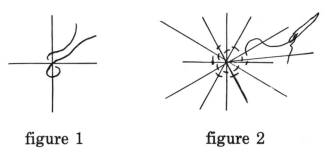

| figure 1 | figure 2 |

Add additional straws to fill in the spaces between these first spokes, tying them in the center as previously described. Cut one straw off just outside the center knot. (This produces the "odd" spoke needed to maintain an over/under weaving pattern.) Begin at the center weaving thread over and under the straws, working outward in a spiral pattern. Continue weaving outward as far as necessary to hold the arrangement securely (see figure 2). Two to four rows of weaving are usually sufficient. Tie off the thread and put a small drop of white glue on the knot to keep it from slipping. Use scissors to trim the end of each straw. Make all straws of even length around the circumference (see figure 3) or cut them to form a patterned edge as desired (see figure 4).

Example:

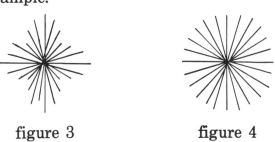

| figure 3 | figure 4 |

SECTION IV:
"Nature Crafts"

Natural materials are used to create works of art.

TOP LEFT: Leaf Skeleton
TOP RIGHT: Sand Painting
BOTTOM: Pebble People

1. LEAF SKELETONS (Shown above, upper left)

A. Materials: You will need fresh green leaves with interesting vein structures, a pad of soft cloths (a folded bath towel works well), a stiff-bristled brush (scrub brush, hair brush, etc.), gold spray paint, glue and colored paper for mounting the completed leaf skeletons.

B. Procedure: Lay the leaf on a pad of soft cloths. Pound it briskly with the stiff bristles of the brush. The object is to puncture many holes in the leaf surface and expose the skeleton-like structure of the veins. This procedure takes patience. At first you will think you are making no progress, but hold the leaf up to the light and you will see the puncture holes. Keep on pounding until almost all of the green portion of the leaf is gone and the vein structure is exposed. (This takes about ten minutes of pounding.)

Spray the finished work with gold paint. (Any other color could be used, but gold is especially effective.) When the paint is dry, glue the leaf skeleton to a sheet of contrasting colored paper for display.

2. SAND PAINTING (Shown on page 103, upper right)

A. Materials: Two or more colors of sand, paintbrush, white glue, a small disposable container, cardboard and old newspapers are needed for this activity.

B. Procedure: Spread newspapers over the work area. In a disposable container, mix the white glue with an equal amount of water.

Draw a picture or design with pencil on the cardboard. It should be simple, with no fine details. Brush thinned glue over one area of the picture. Sprinkle one color of sand over this glued area. (The sand should completely cover the cardboard in that area.) Shake the picture to remove extra sand. Continue in this way, sprinkling sand over one glued area at a time until the entire design is covered with sand. Use different colors of sand in different areas as needed to complete the design.

3. PEBBLE PEOPLE (Shown on page 103, bottom)

A. Materials: Students will need small, smooth pebbles in a variety of shapes and sizes, white glue and florist's clay. Decorative materials may be needed, as described in part B.

B. Procedure: Arrange several pebbles stacked in various ways until the overall shape suggests the form of a human, animal, fish or bird. When a satisfactory arrangement of pebbles is achieved, fasten the pieces together.

Wherever possible, use white glue for joining the pieces together. This provides a sturdy, permanent bond. When this is not possible (when surfaces are rough or slanted), use florist's clay. Put a small wad of florist's clay on one pebble, then press it very firmly against the other pebble.

The construction can be left plain, as shown on page 103, or they can be highly decorated. Clothing, facial features and so on can be painted on or created by gluing on scraps of yarn, cloth, lace, tiny buttons, etc.

4. SEED MOSAICS

A. Materials: Provide heavy cardboard, pencil, white glue and seeds in a variety of sizes, shapes and colors. (Birdseed, fruit pits, corn, dried beans or peas, sunflower seeds, rice, barley — any and all types of seeds can be used.)

B. Procedure: Cut cardboard to the desired size for the picture. Draw on the cardboard the desired picture. It can be realistic or abstract, but should be kept simple.

Spread glue in one section of the picture. Press seeds of one kind into the glued area. Continue in this way, completing one small section of the picture at a time. Use different types of seeds in different areas of the picture for color and texture interest. Keep the picture flat until the glue is thoroughly dry.

5. FOREST FOLKS (Shown on page 107)

A. Materials: White glue, decorative materials such as paint, yarn, fabric scraps, etc., and a collection of natural materials native to your geographic area are needed for this activity. (Collect such things as pine cones, burrs, nuts, bark, seed pods and shells.)

B. Procedure: Only inspiration, not specific directions, can be given for these creations. Every area of the nation has natural materials found there and nowhere else. Every pine cone, rock or shell is different from every other. It is virtually impossible to exactly duplicate any object made from natural materials.

Simply take whatever natural materials you have on hand. Study the pieces carefully until the shape suggests some animal form. An opened milkweed pod may resemble butterfly wings, an unopened pine cone may suggest the form of a fish, a fat pine cone may look like a fluffy owl, and so on. Add whatever decorative pieces are necessary to transform the basic shape into the creature you see in your mind.

In the photograph on page 107, the teddy bear is made from six liquidambar (sweet gum) burrs glued together to form the body. Its ears are pine cone petals, its nose an acorn cap, its eyes

Forest Folks

kernels of dried corn. A bright red ribbon bow was added. The mouse's body is formed from a teasel burr. Its ears are pine cone petals, its eyes are shiny black beads. Notice the whimsical straw flower bouquet held in its twig hands. The turtle is made from a piece of bark with a natural and startlingly realistic turtle-shell pattern. Its legs, tail and head are small stones glued to the underside of the bark. Claw lines and facial features were drawn with a black felt pen.

The possibilities for creating with natural materials are limitless. Take whatever materials are available to you and let your imagination be your guide.

6. FISH FOSSIL PRINTS

A. Materials: Students will need a whole, dead fish, porous white paper (newsprint works well), black India ink and a paintbrush or brayer.

If you do not live in an area where a fish can be caught by the children, you can get one at a meat market. Hundreds of prints can be made from one fish, so several teachers may want to split the cost of the fish and each take turns using it in the classroom. Coordinate this project so all classes use the fish on one day so the fish can be discarded before it gets smelly!

B. Procedure: Lay the fish on a protective layer of old newspapers. Paint the exposed half of the fish with a light coating of India ink. Experience will tell you how much ink is enough. Lay a sheet of white paper over the fish. Gently press down on all areas of the paper, smoothing it across all areas of the fish. Lift off the paper and the design of the fish will be imprinted on it. Re-ink the fish for the next print to be made.

7. THUMB PRINT PICTURES

A. Materials: Provide a stamp pad with black ink, a black fine-line felt pen and small pieces of white drawing paper. (These designs are small and would be lost on large paper. A sheet of standard typing paper cut into four or even six equal parts makes good sized paper for this project.)

B. Procedure: Press your thumb onto the stamp pad, then press your inked thumb onto white paper to print your thumbprint. Look at the design. Does it suggest the form of a bird or animal? Add a very few quick strokes with a fine-line felt pen to make lines suggesting wings, legs, ears, tail, etc., to heighten the realism of the figure. The example shows a baby chick, owl, rabbit, mouse and flying bird made from thumb print designs.

Example:

Practice a variety of designs on scrap paper. Then try making a complete scene incorporating thumb print animal designs. Simple pen lines can be added to suggest grass, trees, clouds, etc., as needed for background features.

8. SPIDER WEB PRINTS

A. Materials: An abandoned spider web (please do not take a spider's current home!), heavy cardboard, black enamel paint, white spray paint, old newspapers and clear spray shellac or fixative are needed for this activity.

B. Procedure: There will not be enough abandoned spider webs available for each child to make his own picture, so this must be a group project making one web picture for classroom display.

Cut a piece of cardboard large enough to serve as a background for the web. Paint the cardboard with black enamel paint and allow the paint to dry thoroughly.

Spread newspapers behind and around the web to mask surrounding areas against paint spray. Spray the web with a fine coat of white paint. While the white paint is still wet, bring the black cardboard up behind and against the web so the web adheres flat against the cardboard. The delicate pattern of the white web is now shown in contrast against the black mounting sheet. When the web has dried thoroughly, spray over the web with clear shellac or fixative for protective coverage.

9. CRYSTAL GARDEN (Shown on page 111, upper left)

A. Materials: For each crystal garden, you will need a shallow, disposable pan (aluminum frozen meat pie pans work well), 2 - 4 charcoal briquettes, a measuring spoon and a mixture of:

3 Tablespoons salt
3 Tablespoons liquid laundry bluing
3 Tablespoons clear ammonia

Liquid food coloring is optional.

B. Procedure: Put the salt, bluing and ammonia into a pan and stir to mix. This solution will have a strong ammonia smell which is irritating to the eyes, nose and throat. Work in a well ventilated room and avoid breathing the fumes as much as possible. (Stir at arm's length with face turned aside.) The fumes will abate in a

UPPER LEFT: Crystal Garden
ALL OTHERS: Painted Rocks

few minutes. Put the charcoal briquettes into the pan and spoon the mixture over them, allowing some of the liquid to absorb into the charcoal. (Spoon 3 - 4 times over each briquette.) Then, let the charcoal stand undisturbed in the pan. Within a few hours, amazingly beautiful crystals will begin to form. By the next day, each briquette will be covered with a delicate, miniature crystal forest. For an even greater appreciation of nature's artistry at work, look at the crystal formations through a magnifying glass.

To keep the crystals growing, make a new salt/bluing/ammonia mixture and pour it into the pan each time the previous mixture is totally absorbed into the charcoal and the pan is dry.

The first mixture will probably be absorbed overnight. The charcoal is now saturated and subsequent mixtures will absorb less quickly (1 - 2 days). The more briquettes in the pan, the quicker the mixture will be absorbed.

Pour the mixture AROUND the briquettes, never directly on them, or the crystals already formed will be destroyed. They will, however, grow back again. Do not touch the crystal formations. They are fragile and will disintegrate. (The "Crystal Garden" shown on page 111 had been growing only 48 hours when the picture was taken.)

C. Variation: Crystals grown as previously directed will be white. To produce colored crystals, set the briquettes in the pan and drop 5 - 6 drops of liquid food coloring onto the top surface of each. Allow the coloring to absorb into the briquettes. Then spoon over the salt/ammonia/bluing mixture as previously directed. Colors will be pale at first, becoming more brilliant as crystals grow larger.

Putting a different color on each briquette in the pan or different colors on different areas of the same briquette, produces fascinating color displays. Use only 2 - 3 drops of each color if more than one color is used on the same briquette.

10. PAINTED ROCKS (Shown on page 111)

A. Materials: Provide rocks of interesting shapes, plus decorative materials as needed. Features may be cut from paper or cloth and pasted in place, painted on with enamel paints or colored felt pens, etc.

B. Procedure: At least a week before working on this project, ask children to be on the lookout for rocks of interesting shapes and to bring them to class before a given day. Ask children to select a rock with "artistic possibilities" — one that can be decorated with paint, felt pens, scraps of fabric or paper to resemble a fish, bird, animal, etc.

The object of this project it NOT to search endlessly for a rock that resembles one of the examples pictured. These rocks are pictured only to demonstrate the wide range of creative possibilities. Encourage each child to take whatever rock he finds and let the shape of that particular rock guide the decorative design.

On the scheduled work day, set out a variety of decorative materials as previously described. Let children select those materials appropriate to decorate their rocks as desired.

In the photograph on page 111, a smooth, rounded stone was painted with high-gloss enamel to look like a ladybug. The wire antennae are secured to the bottom of the rock with masking tape. The footprint shaped work was given "toes" drawn with a felt pen. A felt pen was also used to decorate the three flat stone owls. They are secured to a driftwood base with florist's clay. The fish shaped rock was given a paper reinforcement eye and a cut paper smile.

11. SAND CANDLES

A. Materials: Wax (use old candle stubs, paraffin or commercial candle wax), old crayons, cotton string, a coffee can, pan of water, hot plate and a sturdy box filled with damp sand are needed for this activity. Sand should not be to soggy — only damp enough to hold a molded shape.

SAFETY PRECAUTION: NEVER melt wax in a container set directly over the heat. The wax easily catches on fire.

B. Procedure: Mold a depression in wet sand. Make it the size and shape of the desired candle.

Melt wax by placing it in the coffee can, then setting the can in a pan of water on the hot plate. Use as low a burner setting as possible. Add crayon shavings to the wax to produce the desired color. Dip cotton string into the melted wax and set it aside to dry. This will be used as candle wicking.

Pour the melted wax into the molded depression in the sand. Let it cool and harden. A depression will form in the candle's center. Add more melted wax to fill this depression. When the candle is cool and hard, carefully remove it from the sand. Brush away any loose sand. Sand will be imbedded in the sides and bottom of the candle. This should be left "as is." It provides both decorative and textural interest.

Use a slender nail or ice pick to drive a hole down into the center of the candle. Insert a wick in this hole. Pour a tiny amount of wax around the wick to secure it firmly in place. Candles of larger diameters can be given two or more wicks spaced several inches apart.

12. SNOW CANDLES

A. Materials: Students will need wax (use old candle stubs, paraffin or commercial candle wax), old crayons, cotton string, a metal coffee can, pan of water, hot plate and a cold winter's day when the snow is deep.

B. Procedure: Prepare melted, colored wax and candle wicking as described in "Sand Candles," page 114.

Mold a small depression in the snow, making it the shape of the candle desired, but about half the desired depth and diameter. (If snow is fluffy, sprinkle it with water so it will firmly maintain the molded shape.) Pour melted wax into this molded depression and let it cool and harden. Lift out the hardened shape. Pour a little more wax into the depression in the snow, then set the candle back in place. Pour in additional melted wax around the edges of the hardened wax until the wax level is even with the first shape molded. Let this second pouring of wax cool and harden. Continue in this way until the candle reaches the desired size. The heat from the melted wax will melt snow in the depression, so the mold grows progressively larger with each pouring.

The resulting candle form, viewed from the top, is a series of concentric rings much like those seen in the trunk of a cut tree. You may wish to use different, harmonizing colors of wax for each pouring to accentuate this pattern of concentric rings.

Use a slender nail or ice pick to drive a hole into the center of the completed candle. Insert a wick, then pour a small quantity of wax around the wick to secure it firmly in place. Candles of larger diameters can be given two or more wicks spaced several inches apart.

13. EARTH OBJECTS

A. Materials: Provide sturdy, shallow box lids or Styrofoam meat trays, tempera paint in earth tones, paint brushes, white glue and natural objects; such as stones of interesting color and/or texture, bleached bones (see "Bone Art," page 120 for directions to prepare bones for use in art projects), feathers, seed pods, driftwood, seashells, etc.

B. Procedure: The box lid will become a display frame for a collection of natural objects. Paint the interior and edges of the lid in an earth-tone color that contrasts nicely with the objects to be displayed. Styrofoam meat trays cannot be painted so are used "as is." When the paint is thoroughly dry, arrange the objects in the lid. The objects may be arranged to totally fill the frame, or smaller groupings may be placed on or off center within the frame.

Use one type of material in the display (all rocks or all seed pods for example) or try a combination of materials. Feathers and bones combine nicely in these arrangements, or seashells with driftwood pieces, etc.

Make many trial arrangements until it looks artistically pleasing to you. Then, lift one object at a time, apply glue to the back surface and set it back in place. Continue in this way gluing all objects in place. Allow the lid to lie flat until the glue dries thoroughly. Then the arrangement can be pinned to the bulletin board for display.

This project has two equally important benefits. Children produce interesting art work and they become more aware of the beauty of common natural objects they may have totally overlooked in the past.

The Eyes Have It

14. THE EYES HAVE IT (Shown on page 117)

A. Materials: Natural objects, commercially purchased plastic eyes (available at craft stores), white glue and/or florist's clay are needed for this activity.

B. Procedure: This is a speedy project with startling results. Simply glue plastic eyes onto an object. The object appears to come alive!

The photograph on page 117 shows eyes added to an arrangement of gnarled wood, a rock, two shapes of pine cones and two kinds of seashells. Try putting eyes on a banana, or pear, a leaf or a walnut. No matter what you glue eyes onto, it becomes your new and instant friend!

The size of eyes used as well as their placement (close together or set far apart, high up on the "face" or low) changes the creature's appearance totally. Shift the eyes from place to place to decide where they will give the best effect. If the surface is smooth and flat, apply a dot of glue and set the eye into the glue. Let it sit undisturbed until the glue dries. If the surface is rough or slanted, put a small wad of florist's clay on the back of the eye, then press the eye into place.

15. BONSAI

A. Materials: Students will need a shallow planting container, potting soil, plant scissors, firm but highly pliable wire and young woody plants such as evergreens or shrubs.

Children may bring suitable plants from home or a local nursery may give you stunted, deformed, undersized evergreens or shrubs totally unsaleable but perfect for this project. If obtaining plants is a difficulty, you may prefer to create just one Bonsai for classroom demonstration and display rather than having children work on individual projects.

B. Procedure: Bonsai is the Oriental art form of growing miniature forms of normal trees. For example, a maple tree can be 150 years old and only a foot high. The trees are passed from generation to generation within a family and are highly valued.

Begin with any small sized (about a 1-gallon container size) tree or shrub with several branches. Take it out of the soil and cut off at least half the length of all the roots. Plant it in good soil in a small, shallow container. These two steps hamper root growth and keep the plant stunted and dwarfed. Roots must be re-cut in this same way at least once a year to maintain the miniature size of the plant. Cut away the top growth to give the plant an open, airy appearance. Leave only a few branches with artistic, gnarled character. To emphasize the gnarled shape, wrap wire several times around the main stem and then out along the length of a branch.

Example:

Bend the branch to the desired shape and the wire will hold it in that position. Wire should be firm but not tight enough to cut into the main stem or branch. Wires can be removed once the branch is well established in that position — it may take a year or more.

16. BONE ART (Shown on page 121, left and center)

A. Materials: Begin a collection of chicken, beef and/or lamb bones. (Pork bones are porous and cannot be cleaned well; therefore, for sanitary reasons, they must not be used for this project.) Bones can be saved in plastic bags in the freezer until enough are accumulated for this project. You will also need soap, bleach, glue and heavy tagboard or cardboard for mounting the arrangements.

B. Procedure: To prepare the bones for use, first clean them thoroughly of all scraps of meat, fat or gristle. Use a steel brush and a nut pick for cleaning hard to reach spots. If bones are simmered in water for several hours, they are easier to clean. Wash the bones in hot, soapy water. Whiten the bones by soaking them 2 - 3 hours in a bleach and water solution (1/4 cup bleach to each quart of water), then spread them to dry. They will continue whitening as they dry.

Make many trial arrangements of the bones until you achieve an interesting realistic or abstract design. Glue the bones in place and allow the arrangement to remain undisturbed until the glue is thoroughly dry.

LEFT AND CENTER: Bone Art
RIGHT: Insects-That-Never-Were

17. INSECTS-THAT-NEVER-WERE
(Shown on page 121, right)

A. Materials: Collect small seed pods, burrs, nut shells, acorns, etc., to use as insect bodies, plus twigs for legs or antennae. Collect other suitable natural materials that are available in your area. For example, maple seeds make perfect wings for flies or dragonflies, leaves from a silver dollar plant or milkweed pod halves work well for the wings of butterflies or moths. White glue and florist's clay are needed for fastening the pieces together.

B. Procedure: These are strictly creations of each child's unique imagination. Begin with a large seed pod or nut shell for the main body section. Wisps of straw or small twigs can be glued in place for legs and antennae, small seeds used for eyes, slender leaves for wings, etc.

Specific directions cannot be given, for each creation is unique and uses whatever natural materials are on hand. In the photograph on page 121, the top insect was made from a walnut shell. Rose thorns were glued to the back for spines. Its legs are twigs, its bulging eyes are bright red pyracantha berries. The center insect has an almond shell body, twig legs, sunflower seed and corn kernel eyes, and twig antennae. Its wings are pepper tree leaves. The caterpillar's body was cut from a bottle brush tree branch. Its eyes are corn kernels and its antennea are slender bottle brush leaves.

Wherever possible, use white glue for fastening pieces together. This provides a sturdy, permanent bond. When this is not possible (when surfaces are rough or slanted), use tiny bits of florist's clay for fastening pieces together.

18. PORCUPINES

A. Materials: Students will need whole, raw potatoes, a metal spoon (metal measuring spoons or melon ball scoops work very well), toothpicks or wooden matches, colored thumbtacks, garden soil and grass seed.

B. Procedure: Slice the top (lengthwise) off a whole, raw potato. Use a metal spoon to scoop out the interior of the potato. Leave the side walls at least 1/4 inch thick and hollow down at least 1 inch into the potato. Push four toothpicks or wooden matchsticks into the base of the potato to serve as legs. Push two colored thumbtacks into the front end of the potato to serve as eyes. Fill the hollowed-out area of the potato almost to the brim with garden soil. Press the soil down firmly and smooth out the surface. Scatter grass seed evenly and generously on top of the soil and cover it with a thin layer of soil. Sprinkle the top surface with water and set the potato in a sunny window. Keep the soil damp but not soggy. A plant mist spray bottle works very well for watering the seed. In ten days to two weeks, the grass will sprout. As the grass grows longer, the whole creation assumes the appearance of a grass-spined porcupine.

Example:

19. DRIED ARRANGEMENTS

A. Materials: Provide dried weeds or flowers with long, firm stems, wire mesh (1/4 inch carpenter's mesh works very well), tin snips, work gloves, tape, scissors, string, old newspapers, colored ribbon and spray paint. (While any color paint could be used, gold or white are especially effective.)

B. Procedure: Use tin snips to cut wire mesh to the desired background size. Wear gloves to protect against cuts from sharp wire edges while cutting. Cover the sharp edges of this cut piece of mesh with tape to protect against cuts and to provide a finished border. Arrange the dried weeds or flowers like a bouquet on the mesh. Make several trial arrangements until one pleases you. Tie each piece in the arrangement onto the screen. To do this, simply run a string from the back of the mesh through to the front side coming up right beside a stem. Pass the string over the stem and at least one wire, then back down into the mesh on the other side. Tie the string on the back side of the mesh. Tall-stemmed pieces may require tying in several places to hold them firmly in place.

When all the pieces in the arrangement have been tied in place, set the arrangement on a layer of protective newspapers and spray it with paint in the desired color. For safety's sake, spray outdoors or in a well-ventilated room. Several light coats of paint give better results than one

Example:

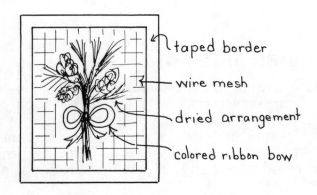

heavy coat. Allow each coat of paint to dry thoroughly before applying the next. When the paint is dry, add a colored ribbon accent. Bring the ribbon up from the back of the mesh, one end on each side of the stem bundle. Tie the ends over the stems and make a bow.

20. FOSSIL PRINTS

A. Materials: Self-hardening clay, a rolling pin, table knife, wide spatula, old newspapers, tempera paint, paintbrush, paper towel or sponge and a collection of natural materials of interesting texture. (Thickly-veined leaves, shells, twigs with interesting branch designs, etc., work very well.)

B. Procedure: Use a rolling pin to roll a flat slab of clay about 1/4 inch thick. Roll in two directions so the slab is of uniform thickness throughout.

Make several trial arrangements of the textured objects on the surface of the clay. When the arrangement pleases you, roll the rolling pin across the top of the objects just hard enough to press their imprints into the clay. Use a table knife to cut out the imprinted section of clay. Remove excess clay scraps from the margins and let the imprinted tile remain in place for about an hour or until the clay hardens somewhat and can be moved without distorting its shape. Use a spatula to move the tile onto a pad of old newspapers. Let it stay undisturbed until it is thoroughly dry. This may take a day or more depending on the dampness of the clay and the room temperature and humidity. Flat tiles must dry slowly, out of direct heat or sunlight or they will warp and crack.

Brush dark colored tempera paint across the surface of the dry tile. Immediately, use a damp paper towel or sponge to wipe across the surface. This will wipe away most of the stain from the flat surface of the tile but leave dark color down in the imprints to highlight the design.

SECTION V:
"In And Out"

Weaving, wrapping and stitchery projects.

UPPER ROW: Twig Weaving (2 examples)
RIGHT CENTER: Wrapped Design
BOTTOM ROW: Waffle Weaving, Circular Loom Weaving

1. TWIG WEAVING (Shown on page 129, top)

A. Materials: Provide branched twigs (taken from dead trees or shrubs — don't injure living plants!), yarn, string, thread or jute, a needle and scissors. Tiny twigs could be woven with fine sewing thread while larger twigs would require correspondingly larger weaving materials.

B. Procedure: Each twig is a totally different design so no exact directions can be given. In general, lay parallel rows of yarn stretching between two arms of the twig (see figure 1). These will be the warp threads. Weave weft threads in and out among these warp threads to create the desired design (see figure 2).

Example:

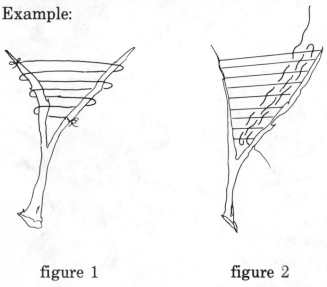

figure 1   figure 2

In the photograph on page 129, notice one design has a very solid, formal appearance while the other has an open and airy feeling. The uniqueness of each twig plus the weaving style chosen by each individual child gives each twig weaving a totally different "personality."

2. WRAPPED DESIGNS (Shown on page 129, right center)

A. Materials: Students will need heavy cardboard, ruler, pencil, scissors, yarn or jute in a variety of colors, white glue and small scraps of felt or colored paper.

B. Procedure: Cut a piece of cardboard about six inches square. Cut away a four inch square from the center of this piece. You now have a one inch wide cardboard "frame."

Roll several colors of yarn or jute into balls about 2 - 3 inches in diameter. Tie an end of one color of yarn to the frame opening, go under the frame on the opposite side, then up and over that side of the frame. Pull the yarn firmly back across the frame opening, go under, up and over the frame on this side. Continue in this way laying down several rows of yarn (see figure 1).

Turn the frame a quarter turn and wrap in the same manner in this new direction (see figure 2).

Example:

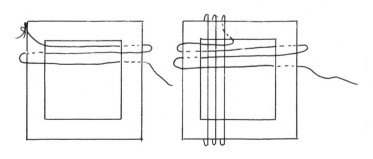

Continue turning the frame a quarter turn after each several rows of wrapping until all four sides of the frame have been worked.

Tie on a new color and work several rows of this new color on each side of the frame. Each successive row is laid close beside the preceding one, working from the outer edges of the frame towards the center. Continue changing colors as desired. When you reach the center, tuck the loose end of yarn under on the back and apply a small drop of white glue to keep it in place.

The four outer corners of the cardboard frame remain exposed. If desired, four 1-inch squares of felt or colored paper can be cut from a color to harmonize or contrast with the wrapping. Glue these squares in place to cover the four exposed corners of the cardboard frame.

3. WAFFLE WEAVING (Shown on page 129, lower left)

A. Materials: Heavy cardboard, scissors and yarn or string are needed for this activity.

B. Procedure: Cut a 6-inch square of cardboard. Cut slots at 3/4 inch intervals along all four sides. Begin by making the first slot in the center of each side. Make the slots deep enough to hold eight strands of yarn.

Make a slit in one corner of the cardboard loom. Tuck the beginning end of yarn into this slit to hold it firmly in place. Thread the loom back and forth as shown in figure 1. Repeat 7 times so that 8 layers of yarn have been placed in each slot.

Example:

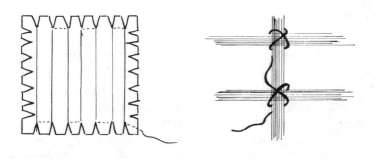

figure 1   figure 2

Next, place 8 layers of yarn in each slot running in the opposite direction. Tie all crossings. Tie a knot around the upper left crossing. Carry this thread down to the crossing directly below. Tie a figure-8 knot at this crossing (see figure 2). Carry the knotting thread to the crossing directly below, tie another figure-8 knot and so on to the lower left crossing. Carry the knotting thread to the next crossing to the right. Tie a figure-8 knot. Move progressively up this row, down the next and so on until you reach the lower right hand corner. After completing the figure-8 knot at this crossing, tie a secure square knot on the back of the work to secure the knotting thread. Carefully, lift the completed work off the cardboard loom. Cut through all loops around the outer edge to create a fringed border.

4. CIRCULAR LOOM WEAVING (Shown on page 129, lower right)

A. Materials: Cardboard and scissors are needed to make the loom. Yarn, string, jute, etc., can be used for the weaving. A yarn needle is also needed.

B. Procedure: Cut a circle of cardboard. Cut away the interior, leaving at least a 1-inch wide circular frame. The frame width should be greater if the loom is cut in a very large diameter. Use a yarn needle to punch an even number of holes evenly around the frame.

Tie a large knot at the end of the warp thread. Thread a yarn needle onto the other end. Bring the warp up through hole #1 and pull until the knot rests firmly against the back of the loom. Bring the thread across the loom and go down in hole #2 and up in #3. Carry the thread across the loom going down into hole #4 and up in #5 (see figure 1). Continue threading warp threads across the loom in this manner.

Example:

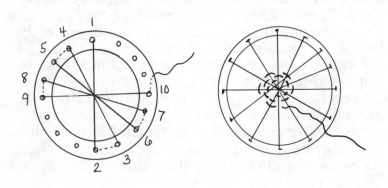

figure 1   figure 2

After threading through all the holes in the loom, bring the thread to the center, wrap it around the crossing threads to secure them and let the loose "tail" of yarn hang at the back of the work. This last thread, running from rim to center, is the "odd" spoke necessary to maintain a constant over-under weaving pattern.

Begin over and under weaving at the center of the loom, spiraling outward toward the edges (see figure 2). When changing colors or upon reaching the end of the weft thread, let loose ends hang at the back of the work. When weaving is completed, weave these loose ends into the back of the work.

Cut the loom away from the finished weaving. If desired, decorative fringe can be tied to each warp loop around the outer edge of the weaving.

5. WEAVING ON A CARDBOARD CONTAINER (Shown on page 136, top)

A. Materials: Small round or square cardboard boxes, pencil, tape measure, yarn needle, white glue, yarn and heavy string or jute are needed for this activity.

B. Procedure: Use a tape measure and pencil to measure and mark placement of dots at 1/2 inch intervals in a row about 1/2 inch from the top and bottom rims of the box (see figure 1). Mark an uneven number of dots along each rim. Use a yarn needle to punch a hole in each of these dots. To create the weaving warp, run yarn in and out through these holes to lay down parallel, vertical lines of yarn (see figure 2). Weave in and out of these warp threads in horizontal rows around the box (see figure 3).

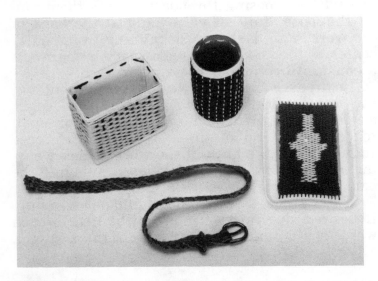

UPPER ROW: Weaving on a Cardboard Container (2 examples)
BOTTOM LEFT: Woven Belt
BOTTOM RIGHT: Weaving in a Styrofoam Tray

Example:

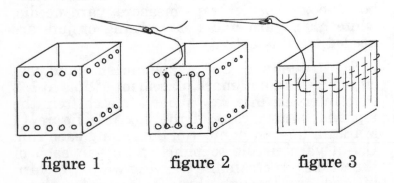

figure 1   figure 2   figure 3

The very top and bottom edges of the box remain uncovered. Spread glue in each of these sections and wrap yarn to fill in these spaces

6. WOVEN BELT (Shown on page 136, lower left)

A. Materials: Students will need jute or macrame cord in two different colors (the belt shown on page 136 was done in rust and natural jute) and a belt buckle. Children can bring worn out or outgrown belts from home, cut off the belt and use the buckle for this project.

B. Procedure: Cut two lengths of cord from two colors (four lengths in all). Each cord should be about four times longer than the desired belt length.

STEP ONE: Hook the buckle on a nail and drape four strands of cord over the buckle alternating colors as shown in figure 1. Pull the cords so all ends are even. (It is easiest to learn this method by keeping the buckle flat on the table.)

Fig. 1

STEP TWO: Take the back strip of cord on the far left side and bring it in front of the same piece of cord hanging in front of the buckle. Moving towards the right, take in turn, each remaining cord hanging in back of the buckle bring each in front of the same strip which hangs in front of the buckle and weave it across to the left.

Fig. 2

STEP THREE: Take the far upper left cord and weave it in and out to the center. Take the far upper right cord and weave it in and out to the center. Continue alternately taking each outside cord from the left and right side and weaving it to the center until the belt reaches the desired length.

Fig. 3

STEP FOUR: To finish off the belt end, take each cord, bring it to the underside and weave it in and out of several woven loops to keep it in place. Cut off the remaining ends.

Fig. 4

Fig. 5

STEP FIVE: Make a braided loop and fasten it in place about three inches back from the buckle.

The woven belt shown on page 136 was woven exactly as previously described except six strands, rather than four, were used in the weaving.

7. WEAVING IN A STYROFOAM TRAY
(Shown on page 136, lower right)

A. Materials: Provide Styrofoam meat trays, scissors, ruler, yarn needle and yarn, string, jute, etc., for the weaving.

B. Procedure: Carefully, push a tip of the scissors through the center of the Styrofoam meat tray. Cut away the center section to make a 1 1/2 - 2 inch (3.5 - 5 cm) wide Styrofoam frame. (See the frame pictured on page 136.)

Use a ruler to guide placement for holes along the top and bottom margins of the frame. Because the edges of the frame are raised, you cannot get a ruler into the frame, so lay it underneath with the markings showing along the frame's inner rim (see example). There must be an odd number of evenly-spaced holes. Puncture the holes with a yarn needle.

Example:

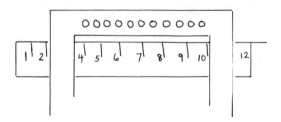

Thread the needle with yarn. Tie a knot in the yarn's end and bring the needle up from the bottom through a hole on the outer edge of the frame. Go across the frame and down in the outer hole on that side of the frame. Come up in the hole right beside it, go across the frame and down in the outer hole on that side of the frame.

Come up in the hole right beside it, go across the frame and down into the hole right beside the first one used. Continue in this way threading the yarn back and forth across the loom through all punched holes. Tie off the remaining end of yarn.

The Styrofoam loom is fragile. Handle the work carefully, trying not to bend it or it will break. Also, keep the warp thread pulled firm but not tight enough to pull out of the frame.

Use yarn threaded on a yarn needle to weave over and under these warp threads to produce the desired pattern of weaving. When the weaving is completed, it may be displayed in the frame as shown on page 136. Or, the frame may be broken away and the weaving removed. In this case, you may wish to add decorative fringe to the edge of the weaving.

8. TAPESTRIES

A. Materials: Heavy corregated cardboard, scissors and yarn or string are needed for this activity.

B. Procedure: Cut a cardboard frame. The interior of the frame will be the size of the finished work. Keep it quite small (under six inches) as this work is slow and a larger piece may cause discouragement. Cut a slit at the upper left and lower right of the frame. These will hold the beginning and ending strands of the warp thread. Wrap yarn around the front and back of the loom.

Example:

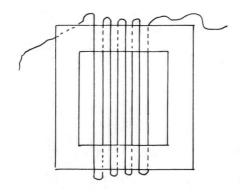

Thread a yarn needle with yarn and weave over and under for two rows across the bottom to hold the work firm. Include warp threads from both the back and front of the loom in this weaving. Do all remaining rows in tapestry stitch, working from the bottom toward the top of the loom. In tapestry stitch, the weft thread passes under, over and then back under each warp thread before moving on to the next.

Example:

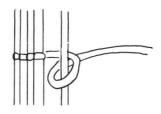

Whenever you reach the end of a weft thread or change colors, let loose ends of thread hang at the back of the work without knotting. When the work is complete, these loose ends can be woven into the work on the back side.

The completed tapestry can be left on the loom for display. Or the loom can be cut away and a stick threaded through the loops at the top and bottom of the work. A hanging loop can be tied onto the outer edges of the top stick.

9. HEDDLE LOOM WEAVING

A. Materials: Students will need eight tongue depressors or Popsicle sticks, strong glue, stout cord or string, colored yarn or jute, a hook, safety pin and a round stick.

B. Procedure: First, make a weaving heddle by gluing and tying together the Popsicle sticks as shown in the illustration. Drill a hole in the center of each vertical stick.

Example:

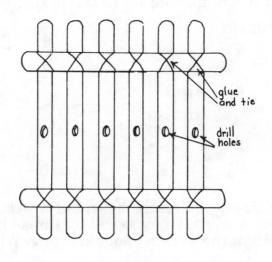

Thread the loom, tie one string, about ten inches longer than the finished belt length desired, to a hook. Pass this string through the hole in the center of one end Popsicle stick and tie it to the round stick. Tie a second string to the hook and pass it through the space between the end stick and the one next to it. Continue threading through each hole and space in the heddle.

Tie the stick to the weaver's waist. To weave, alternately raise and lower the heddle, weaving yarn through the space in the warp strings each time. The weaver winds the completed work around the stick at his waist as he works. He will be moving progressively closer to the hook as work progresses.

Example:

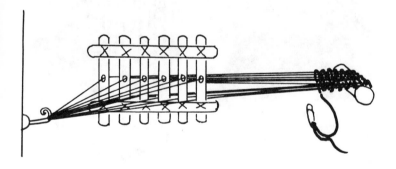

When the weaving is completed, remove it from the loom. Loose ends can be tied together in groups to make fringe or individual threads can be woven back into the weaving on the back side to make straight ends.

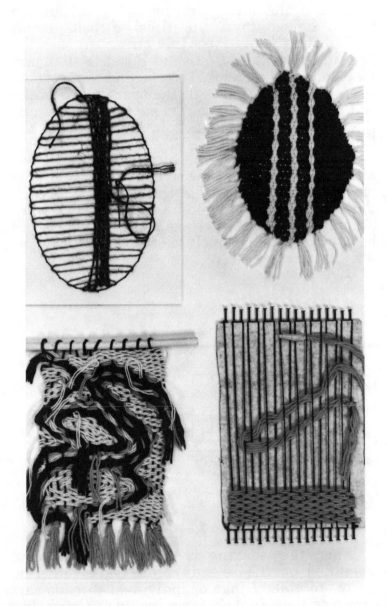

TOP ROW: Loom and Completed Freeform Weaving
BOTTOM ROW: Loom and Completed Speedy Weaving

10. WEAVING FREE-FORM SHAPES
(Shown at top of page 144)

A. Materials: Heavy cardboard, pencil, stout string, yarn or jute, a yarn needle and scissors are needed for this activity.

B. Procedure: On the cardboard, draw the outline of the desired shape. Mark dots at 1/2-inch intervals all along this outline drawing. Use stout string threaded on a yarn needle to stitch in and out in each marked dot (see figure 1). There is now a stitch between every other dot and an empty space between every other dot. Repeat the process to place stitches in each empty space (see figure 2). These are the binding stitches.

Example:

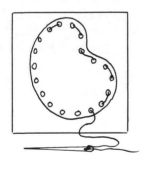   

figure 1   figure 2

Place warp threads running in one direction, anchoring them in the binding stitches (see figure 3). Weave yarn in and out of the warp threads, running the yarn under the binding stitches at each edge to secure them (see figure 4).

Example:

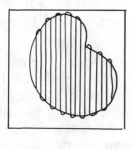

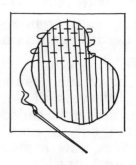

figure 3   figure 4

To remove the finished weaving from the loom, cut each binding stitch on the back side of the cardboard loom. Lift the weaving off the loom and pull away any segments of binding threads that remain caught in the borders of the weaving.

11. SPEEDY WEAVING (Shown at bottom of page 144)

A. Materials: Provide heavy corregated cardboard, nails of a diameter to fit snugly into the corregation "tunnels" at each cut edge of the cardboard, stout string, jute and/or yarn in a variety of weights and colors, masking tape and scissors.

B. Procedure: Cut corregated cardboard about an inch wider than the finished weaving size desired. The edges of the cardboard showing exposed corregation "tunnels" will be the top and bottom edges of the loom. Slip nails into the corregation tunnels along the top and bottom edges. (Nails should be spaced about 1/2 inch apart.) There must be an uneven number of nails along each edge. Use these nails to anchor warp threads running in vertical rows across the face of the loom. The loom completed through this stage and ready for use is pictured on page 144.

Wrap masking tape around the end of a weaving yarn. This stiffens the end of the yarn and serves as a "needle" to help weave the yarn in and out among the warp threads. Individual strands may be woven singly across the warp, or bundles of yarn can be wrapped at the tip with tape and woven across as a single unit. Variation in yarn thickness (single strands or bundles of various thicknesses) creates textural interest in the finished work.

Tie the end of the weft yarn to the first warp thread it will pass over or under. Let the loose end hang at the FRONT of the work. Weave weft threads in and out among the warp threads to create the desired pattern. When the strand or bundle has passed under and over the last desired warp thread, tie those weaving strands in an overhand knot around the warp thread again letting the loose ends hang at the FRONT of the work. The loose ends can be trimmed to a pleasing fringe length when the weaving has been completed.

To remove the weaving from the loom, simply slip the nails out. A slender stick can be threaded through the loops at the top and/or bottom of the finished work or fringe may be tied onto these loops.

The photograph on page 144 shows a completed Speedy Weaving project. A stick was threaded through the top of the work and fringe tied along the bottom edge.

12. WEAVING ON A HANGING LOOM

A. Materials: Students will need a stick, heavy string or cord, yarn, jute, etc., heavy weights (such as bolts, washers, etc.) and scissors.

B. Procedure: Tie a series of evenly spaced cords onto a stick. (There must be an uneven number of cords.) Suspend the stick from a chair back, door handle, fence rail or any convenient spot so the cords hang straight and unobstructed. Tie a heavy weight to the end of each of these warp cords (see figure 1).

Example:

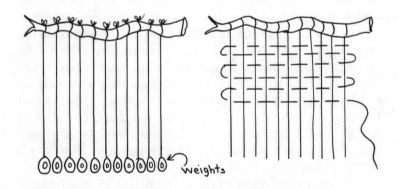

figure 1   figure 2

Begin weaving cords in and out among these hanging warp cords. The heavy weights will keep the warp cords in straight parallel alignment. It is easier to begin weaving at the top of the loom, close to the stick, working progressively downward (see figure 2).

When weaving is completed, untie the weights from the bottom of each warp cord. These loose ends can be grouped into bundles of 3 - 4 strands each and tied in overhand knots, then trimmed to even lengths for fringe. Tie a cord to each end of the stick to serve as a hanging loop. This weaving method is especially well suited for making very large sized wall hangings.

13. HOOKED PICTURES

A. Materials: Medium weight cardboard, pencil, ruler, scissors, slender nail, crochet hook, crayon or felt pen and yarn in many colors are needed for this activity.

B. Procedure: Cut a piece of cardboard about 2 inches longer and 2 inches wider than the desired picture size. Draw a 1-inch margin on all four sides of the tagboard. In the center section (within the 1 inch margins), measure and draw paralled vertical lines spaced about 1/4 inch apart. Measure and draw parallel horizontal lines spaced about 1/4 inch apart. Push a slender nail through every line intersection. The nail holes should be large enough to pass the crochet hook through.

Use a crayon or felt pen to color a design pattern on the "holey" area of cardboard. Hold yarn under the cardboard. Push the crochet hook through one hole (see figure 1). Pull up a loop of yarn. The loop should stand about 1/4 inch above the top cardboard surface (see figure 2).

Example:

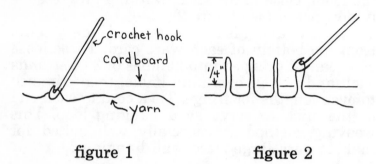

figure 1   figure 2

Pull a yarn loop through every punched hole in the cardboard changing yarn colors as needed to follow the planned pattern. To finish, use the crochet hook to pull up to the top surface any loose "tails" of yarn. Trim these ends even with the loops. DO NOT CUT THE LOOPS.

14. CROSS STITCH DESIGNS (Shown at top of page 151)

A. Materials: Students will need graph paper, pencil, checked fabric, embroidery floss, needle, embroidery hoop and scissors.

B. Procedure: Use graph paper to plan the design, filling in squares to create the desired pattern. Use this plan to guide cross stitch embroidery done within squares of checked fabric. The design can be geometric, abstract or realistic.

In the photograph on page 151, threads from the margins of the fabric were pulled to produce a fringed border. If desired, the finished piece can be stapled to a firm cardboard backing sheet. Glue a paper frame on top.

TOP: Cross Stitch Design
CENTER: Pillow Ticking Patterns
BOTTOM: Designs by the Yard (2 examples)

15. PILLOW TICKING PATTERNS (Shown on page 151, center)

A. Materials: Students will need striped pillow ticking (the same idea can be used on any striped fabric), embroidery floss, embroidery needles, embroidery hoop and scissors.

B. Procedure: In each strip of the pillow ticking, make a single pattern of repeated embroidery stitches. Each row should have a stitch to contrast in color or texture with those on each side of it.

The photograph on page 151 shows one pillow ticking design "under construction" while the other has been completed and framed.

16. DESIGNS BY THE YARD (Shown on page 151, bottom row)

A. Materials: Provide printed fabric, embroidery floss and/or yarn, yarn needle and/or embroidery needle, embroidery hoop and scissors.

B. Procedure: Use the pattern printed on fabric (floral or geometric designs work especially well) as an embroidery design. Use floss or yarn colors to match the fabric colors as closely as possible. Fill in areas of the design with satin stitch, outline borders with couching stitch or backstitch, create stitched texture patterns in colors to contrast with solid colored areas, etc. (The entire fabric need not be covered with embroidery stitches. Simply highlight some areas to create interesting texture variations and to emphasize one or more aspects of the design.) Two children working with identical fabric will produce two totally different products, for each will emphasize different areas of the design with different stitchery patterns.

In the photograph on page 151, black yarn in backstitch was used to outline the floral pattern. French knots in white yarn give additional texture interest. In the Polynesian print, the central geometric figure is totally covered with satin stitch in black embroidery floss.

To display these designs, pin the fabric to the bulletin board, then pin a paper frame over it. Or, stretch and staple the fabric to a heavy cardboard backing sheet, then glue a paper frame on top.

SECTION VI:

"Creating With Clay"

All projects in this chapter are hand built, using self-hardening or non-hardening clay. No special tools or equipment are needed.

To conserve space, basic information and techniques are outlined in the first few pages. Individual projects refer back to these pages so directions need not be endlessly repeated. Please read all this information before beginning any of the construction projects.

The first few projects give children a chance to simply feel and handle clay. No special skills are needed. The next projects introduce techniques for slab-rolling and surface texturing. Later, projects provide practice in joining clay bodies together to create more complex constructions.

Thus, by progressing through this carefully selected series of projects, children can master most of the basic hand-construction skills needed in working with clay.

WORKING WITH CLAY

All projects in this chapter can be hand built of self-hardening or non-hardening clay. No potter's wheel or kiln is required. Because no special tools or equipment are needed, these projects can be used in any classroom. (If you do have a kiln, use firable clay and construct any of these projects exactly as directed. Fire and glaze the completed work according to directions for the particular type of clay used.)

Self-hardening clay has some distinct disadvantages. It cannot be used to create objects which will come in contact with water or moisture of any kind. If dampened, the hardened clay will become moist and pliable again. Also, the dried objects must be handled with care, for unfired clay is brittle and easily broken.

Store clay in tightly sealed plastic bags to keep it moist. If work is interrupted before a project is completed, put the project in a sealed plastic bag and it will stay moist and pliable until work is resumed.

All unfired clay scraps can be salvaged for re-use. Knead together any moist scraps and form them into a smooth ball. Store this ball of clay in a sealed plastic bag. Dry scraps can be placed in a bowl or pail and covered with water. Let it stand several hours or overnight. Drain off the water (outdoors, not down a sink drain!) and put the clay on a thick pad of newspapers. Let it dry several hours or overnight, turning it over several times and changing it to a dry paper pad, until it is no longer sticky and soggy. Knead it into a smooth ball and store it in a sealed plastic bag.

ROLLING A CLAY SLAB

A non-stick work surface is essential for successful results in rolling clay slabs. Old fashioned, heavy oilcloth has a back surface textured like linen or burlap fabric. If you can find this material, cut large rectangles of it (about 12 by 18 inches, 30.5 by 46 cm) and let children use this, shiny side down, as a work surface. (Much oilcloth produced today is thin with a smooth back surface and is not suitable for this use.) Or, stretch cotton fabric (old sheets cut to size work very well) across a smooth board approximately 12 by 18 inches (30.5 by 46 cm). Tack the cotton to the back of the board to hold it firmly in place. The smooth cotton provides an excellent non-stick work surface. A thick pad of newspapers can be used as a last resort. The surface is non-stick, but the paper tends to wrinkle and/or tear with use. Refold the paper to expose a new, clean, dry surface as needed.

Put a smooth ball of clay on the work surface. Press and roll it with a common kitchen rolling pin to form a flat slab about 3/8 inch thick. Roll in two or more directions so the slab is of even thickness throughout. If clay is not of uniform thickness, it will dry unevenly causing it to warp or crack.

ALLOW FOR SHRINKAGE

Clay shrinks as it dries. Every type of clay shrinks differently. Some clays shrink as much as 20% (a pot made 5 inches tall would shrink to 4 inches tall when dry) so allowance must be made for this fact. To test the shrinkage rate of any type of clay, roll a slab and cut out a strip. Measure the length of the strip wet and again when it is thoroughly dry to determine the percentage of shrinkage. Then you will know that to make a pot 5 inches tall you will have to construct it that percentage larger to allow for shrinkage.

When clay is molded around a solid object (as in "Cylinder Pots" page 170), that object MUST be removed before the clay dries. Otherwise, as the clay dries it will press in so tightly the object in the center cannot be removed at all. The pressure may also cause the clay to crack or break entirely.

JOINING CLAY TOGETHER

You have no doubt had the experience of constructing a clay figure, then having the head or arms fall off when the clay dries. Proper sealing of joints will prevent this common mishap.

Joints are made in two steps:

1. SCORE AND SLIP: Mark the area where the two pieces of clay will join together. Use the tines of a fork (or any pointed tool) to scratch cross-hatch lines into the clay in those areas. (The scratches should not be deep.) The object is simply to roughen the surface. This process is called scoring the clay. Dip your finger in water and pat gently across the scored surface. Water will collect in the grooves. Some clay from the sculptured piece will automatically mix with the water. This muddy, clay/water mixture is called slip. It acts much like glue. Firmly press the two scored and slipped pieces together. Small amounts of slip will ooze from the seam. This creates a suction-like force holding the two pieces together.

2. REINFORCE THE JOINT: Roll a slender rope of clay. Lay it along the seam line of the joint. Use a cuticle stick or other pointed tool to press the center section of this rope into the seam line. Use your slightly dampened fingers or a damp cotton swab to smooth clay from this rope onto the surfaces on each side of the joint. This step further welds the two pieces together. When this step is completed, the seam line is smooth and totally invisible.

DRYING CLAY OBJECTS

Allow clay to dry slowly, out of direct heat or sunlight. If clay dries too quickly or unevenly (one portion dries before another), it will warp and/or crack. Whenever possible, rotate drying objects twice daily. This allows all surfaces to have equal exposure to air.

When a clay pot has dried to "leather-hard" stage (still moist but firm enough to hold its shape), turn it upside down. Allow it to finish drying in this position. Clay slabs, such as the "Texture Samplers" described on page 165, need extra care in drying to prevent warpage. When the clay is leather-hard, set it up on some kind of prop so air can circulate on all sides. Flat rulers placed at intervals under the slab work well. Any other flat wooden slats — or even pencils could be used to hold the slab up off the table. Turn slabs over each morning and afternoon until drying is complete.

Drying time for clay pieces varies greatly. The amount of moisture in the clay, the thickness of the clay, the temperature and humidity in the room are all factors. Allow 2 - 7 days for total drying. Clay lightens in color as it dries. You will soon learn to judge dryness by clay color.

CLEAN UP

Set out a pail of water. Let children clean their hands and/or tools in this water first before using the sink. If they clean up directly in the sink, large amounts of clay will go down the drain and harden, thus blocking the drain. Pour the pail of clay water outdoors and use a hose or outdoor tap to clean the pail.

Scraps of clay can be wrapped in newspaper and thrown in the trash, never rinsed down the drain. Or they can be salvaged for re-use (see "Working With Clay," page 157).

TOP ROW: Texture Sampler, Decorating With Non-Hardening Clay
BOTTOM ROW: Coil Design Bowl, Clay Stamps

1. COIL DESIGNED BOWL (Shown on page 161, lower left)

A. Materials: Provide a bowl to use as a mold, newspapers, paper towels or a sponge, a shallow pan of water, tempera paint, brush and self-hardening clay.

B. Procedure: Line the bowl with a single layer of newspaper. This keeps clay from sticking to the bowl.

Roll lumps of clay between the palm of your hand and the table top to create ropes of clay somewhat thicker than a pencil. Roll lengths of this rope to form tight coils the size of half dollars or silver dollars.

Example:

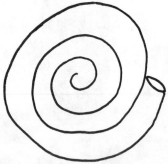

Set one coil in the center bottom of the paper-lined mold. Set more coils in a ring around this center one. Continue working upward in the bowl laying coils tightly together against the sides of the bowl until you reach the rim.

There will be small open spaces where coils do not fit exactly against each other. Roll smooth balls of clay and stuff them into these openings to fill them completely. Use short lengths of clay rope or balls of clay to fill in along the top edge so the clay is even with the rim of the bowl. Smooth the clay with your moistened fingers to create a smooth top rim. Use your moistened fingers to smooth the entire interior of the clay bowl. Work until the surface is as smooth as possible and no coil designs are visable. This welds all pieces together.

Let the work sit undisturbed about an hour, or until the clay is firm enough to hold its shape. Then, invert the bowl and pull gently on the newspapers between the bowl and clay to remove the clay from the mold. Pull off newspapers adhering to the clay. The coil design appears on the outside surface of the bowl while the interior is smooth. Leave the bowl upside down until it is thoroughly dry. Then paint it inside and out with tempera paint. (Brown or terra cotta colors look most natural.) Immediately, use a damp sponge or paper towel to wipe away the paint. The paint color will now be lighter on the smooth raised surfaces and dark in the cracks to accent the coil design. (The bowl on page 161 is shown upside down to better display the coil-patterned exterior surface.)

2. DECORATING WITH NON-HARDENING CLAY (Shown on page 161, upper right)

A. Materials: Students will need non-hardening clay and bottles or jars. Non-hardening clay has an oil base and will stay soft and pliable indefinitely, even when exposed to air. DO NOT USE HARDENING CLAY. As it dries, it will shrink away from the container and fall off.

Ceramic bottles were used for the projects shown on page 161. Clear or colored glass bottles or jars of any shape could be used.

B. Procedure: Wash jars or bottles thoroughly, removing all paper labels. (Make sure the bottles are totally dry before proceeding.) Then, simply roll, coil, pinch or press non-hardening clay to create the desired decorative shapes. Press the shapes firmly against the bottle to anchor them in place to form an overall decorative design. The entire bottle can be covered or only a portion of it as shown on page 161. Using clay of several different colors adds interest to the completed design. The decorated bottles may be used as vases, weed pots, brush or pencil holders, etc.

3. CLAY STAMPS (Shown on page 161, lower right)

A. Materials: Clay, old newspapers and carving tools such as yarn needles, slender nails, cuticle sticks, nut picks, etc., are needed for this activity.

B. Procedure: Clay stamps are used for decorating moist clay. Their imprints are shown on projects throughout this chapter. To use the stamp, simply press it into moist clay to imprint its design. The dried stamp will not stick to moist clay and it can be stored for use over and over again.

To make a clay stamp, first protect the work surface with a folded sheet of newspaper. Set a golf ball sized lump of clay on the paper. Roll the clay between the palm of your hand and the table top to make a solid cylinder about 1 inch in diameter (thicker for large stamps, thinner for small ones) and about 3 inches long. Thump one end of the cylinder against the table several times to make that end perfectly flat and smooth. Use any appropriate tools to cut or press a design into that smooth surface. The design should stand in relief, about 1/4 inch higher than the carved-away background. Pinch the opposite end of the cylinder to make it more slender than the stamp end. This is so the stamp can be held easily during use. Let the stamp dry thoroughly and it is ready for use.

4. TEXTURE SAMPLER (Shown on page 161, upper left)

A. Materials: Provide clay, rolling pin, oil-cloth, knife and a variety of texturing materials as described below.

B. Procedure: Texturing moist clay surfaces is a basic clay-working skill. This activity gives awareness and practice in that skill. Texturing skills learned here will be used in projects throughout this chapter.

Roll a clay slab about 3/8 inch thick (see page 158 for slab rolling directions). Cut out a rectangle, then mark the rectangle into areas of interesting size and shape. (A ruler edge pressed into the clay works well for marking off areas.)

Use common objects pressed into the clay to texture various areas of the slab. Press buttons, pencil points, paper clips, rough stones, highly textured bark, lace, etc., into the clay, one item per area, to see the imprints they make. The object is to test as many texturing tools as possible.

The patterns in the sample shown on page 161 were made with scissor tips, the end of a slender dowel rod, the edge of a matchbook, a toothbrush and the tip of a teaspoon.

Let the slab dry thoroughly, (see "Drying Clay Objects," page 160 for special instructions for drying clay slabs with minimum warpage.) Let children show their completed samplers and tell how each pattern was created. This increases every child's awareness of the almost limitless possibilities for texture designs in clay.

5. RECTANGULAR POTS

A. Materials: Students will need clay, oilcloth, ruler, a rolling pin and a table knife.

B. Procedure: Roll a slab of clay about 3/8 inch thick (see page 158 for slab rolling directions). Cut out a square or rectangular piece of any desired size to use as the pot base.

Cut each side piece of any desired height. The length of each piece should equal one side of the pot base MINUS 3/8 inch (the thickness of the clay). If you wish to texture the pot walls, do it now while pieces are lying flat. Allow all the pieces to lie flat and undisturbed until the clay dries just enough to firmly hold its shape when handled.

Each wall piece is set ON TOP OF, not beside, the base section. Wall sections overlap at corners as shown in the example. This placement gives the greatest possible strength to the construction.

Example:

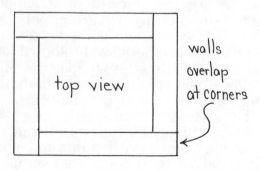

top view

walls
overlap
at corners

Score and slip the edges of each piece where it will join onto another (see "Score and Slip" directions on page 159). Press each piece firmly into place. Reinforce all joints both inside and outside the pot (see page 159 for directions to reinforce joints).

6. STEAM ROLLERS (Shown on page 168, lower left)

A. Materials: Clay, a rolling pin, oilcloth, a table knife and old newspapers are needed for this activity. Tempera paint and brushes are optional.

B. Procedure: Refer to the photograph on page 168 for a concept of this finished product. These creatures are called "Steam Rollers" because the poor fellows look as if they had just been run over by one!

Protect the work surface with newspapers. Roll a slab of clay about 3/8 inch thick (see page 158 for slab rolling directions). Use a table knife to cut out three to five free-form human shapes about 6 to 8 inches tall. You may wish to cut a paper pattern for the figures or simply cut them free hand. Think of it as cutting gingerbread men from rolled cookie dough — its the same idea. Carefully, remove all cut-away scraps leaving the "men" in place on the table. Let them dry undisturbed about 1/2 hour. (The clay should still be very moist and pliable and bend without cracking, but firm enough so the figures will not stretch out of shape when moved.)

Use your moistened finger tips to smooth any rough edges. Bend the figures into acrobatic shapes. Drape them over tin cans or cardboard

**TOP ROW: Cylinder Construction, Lanterns
BOTTOM ROW: Steam Rollers, Conesville**

tubes, prop them with newspaper wads or books — use any appropriate materials for supporting the figures in the desired position while the clay dries thoroughly. The dried figures may be painted a solid color with tempera paint or left in their natural clay color. Arrange the figures in groupings for display.

7. CONESVILLE (Shown on page 168, lower right)

A. Materials: Provide clay and various decorative materials as described.

B. Procedure: Roll a small ball of clay (about walnut size) and press it down over your thumb to make a cone-shaped "thimble." This will be the body of the figure. Press a dent in the thimble top. Roll a ball of clay a little less than 1 inch in diameter. This will be the figure's head. Scratch the thimble top and one side of the small clay ball with a toothpick to roughen the surfaces. Dampen these rough surfaces lightly with water. Press the roughened surface of the clay ball firmly down into the depression in the thimble. Roll a slender rope of clay and wrap it around the neck joint. Smooth this clay up onto the head and down onto the body to form a solid, smooth joint. Slender ropes of clay attached at shoulder level form the two arms. Arrange them in the desired positions, then press the lower ends to form hand shapes and to adhere the hands to the body. Use a toothpick to make indentations creating separate fingers and to etch clothing outlines and decorations. A pencil point can be used to press in eyes and other desired facial features.

Allow the figures to dry completely. The clay can now be stained or painted with tempera or oil base paint. A light coat of clear shellac protects the paint and gives the finished figure a dull gloss. The figures shown on page 168 are in their natural clay color.

8. CYLINDER POTS (Shown on page 168, upper left)

A. Materials: Students will need clay, rolling pin, oilcloth, table knife, newspapers and masking tape. Cylinders are formed around a cylinder-shaped mold. Tin cans, cardboard tubes, oatmeal boxes, etc., can be used as molds.

B. Procedure: Select a can or tube the size of the desired cylinder pot. Cover the can with a single layer of newspaper taped in place with masking tape. The paper prevents clay from sticking to the mold.

Roll a slab of clay about 3/8 inch thick (see page 158 for slab rolling directions). Cut a piece the height of the mold and the length of the mold's diameter. If you wish to texture the clay wall, do it now while the piece is lying flat. The cylinder pot shown on page 168 was textured with the tines of a fork. The swag is a slender rope of clay laid in place, then pressed along each side with the tip of a nut pick. This not only added design features, but also firmly fastened the swag to the clay wall.

Score and slip each end of the slab (see page 159 for "Score and Slip" directions). Roll the slab around the mold, pressing ends firmly together. Reinforce this joint as described on page 159.

Set the clay cylinder, with mold still inside, onto the clay slab. Cut around the cylinder to make a base of perfectly matched size. Remove clay scraps from around this cut-out circle. Lift off the cylinder. Score and slip (see page 159) areas where the cylinder and base will join together. Press the cylinder, with mold still inside, down onto the base. Reinforce the outside base joint as directed on page 159.

Allow the construction to stand undisturbed until the clay is "leather-hard" (still moist and somewhat pliable, but firm enough to hold its shape when handled). Remove the center mold. Reinforce all joints on the interior of the pot. Turn the pot upside down to dry thoroughly.

9. LANTERNS (Shown on page 168, upper right)

A. Materials: Clay, rolling pin, oilcloth, table knife, cylinder-shaped mold and a votive candle are needed for this activity.

B. Procedure: Roll a clay slab about 3/8 inch thick (see page 158 for slab rolling directions). Cut pieces for a cylinder as described in the activity "Cylinder Pots," page 170.

While the wall section still lies flat on the table top, cut a series of holes of any shape in the clay. You can cut circles, squares, slots — whatever shape opening is desired.

In the lanterns pictured on page 168, one has been cut with V-shaped notches. These shapes were then pushed out, with tips curled downward. Rectangular slots were cut in the other pot. The cut-out pieces were fastened to the wall between openings for additional design.

Assemble the pieces as described in "Cylinder Pots," page 170. When the clay is dry, set a votive candle inside to complete the lantern.

10. PENDANT (Shown on page 173, upper right)

A. Materials: Provide clay, rolling pin, non-stick work surface (a pad of newspapers works well for this small project), a table knife and clay stamps (see page 164) or common household items to press or cut decorative, textured patterns into the pendant. Various coloring materials and cord for hanging are also needed.

B. Procedure: Use a rolling pin to roll a small clay slab about 1/4 inch thick. From the slab, cut a small geometric or abstract shape. The shape should be approximately silver dollar size or smaller. Clay is heavy and a larger pendant would be uncomfortable to wear. Use a clay stamp (see page 164) or household items for pressing or cutting designs into the disc. Use a nail or slender knitting needle to puncture two hanging holes at the top of the pendant. Using two hanging holes, rather than one, allows the pendant to hang flat when worn. Smooth any rough edges with your moistened finger tips. Allow the disc to dry thoroughly.

The pendant can be colored in many different ways. Paint it solidly with one color of tempera paint, then immediately use a damp paper towel or sponge to wipe away the color. The color will now be pale on smooth, raised surfaces and dark in indented areas to accent the design. Areas of the disc can also be painted with different colors of tempera or oil based paint, then coated with clear shellac when the paint is dry.

Use a length of leather thong or any other type of string threaded through the two holes at the top of the pendant to complete the necklace. The pendant shown on page 173 is hung on a dark brown shoelace.

LEFT: Mobile
TOP RIGHT: Pendant
BOTTOM RIGHT: Weed Pot

11. MOBILES (Shown on page 173, left)

A. Materials: Students will need clay, rolling pin, oilcloth, table knife, string or cord, nails, tempera paint, brushes and driftwood or gnarled branches from which to suspend the mobiles.

B. Procedure: Roll a slab of clay about 3/8 inch thick (see page 158). Use a table knife to cut shapes from the clay. Cut about 7 - 9 shapes, none larger than 4 inches. Shapes of fish, birds, leaves, mushrooms and the like work especially well for this project. Carefully remove all cutaway scraps leaving the shapes undisturbed on the table. Allow them to dry about ½ hour, or until the clay is firm enough to hold its shape when handled.

Use your moistened finger tips to smooth any rough edges. Cut or press decorative designs or textures in the clay using such objects as nails, toothpicks, sticks, etc., as needed. Design both sides of each piece, as the mobile will turn and both sides of each piece can be seen. Run a nail or slender knitting needle through the thickness of each piece to make a hanging hole (see figure 1). REMOVE THE NAILS. (Clay will shrink around the nails as it dries, making the nails impossible to remove later.) Allow the pieces to dry thoroughly.

Paint each piece all over with tempera paint. (Brown or terra cotta colors look most natural.) Immediately, use a damp sponge or paper towel to wipe the surfaces. Raised, flat surfaces will now be pale colored while colors remain dark in the indentations to accent the design.

String the pieces on lengths of cord putting a knot below each piece to keep it from slipping down the cord (see figure 2). Hang several strings from a single piece of driftwood, bark or a gnarled branch. Suspend the completed mobile where it is free to turn and swing in the breeze.

Example:

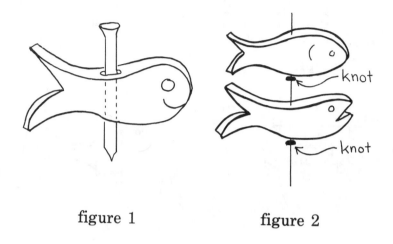

figure 1   figure 2

12. WEED POT (Shown on page 173, lower right)

A. Materials: Self-hardening clay, oilcloth, a rolling pin, a table knife, paper and scissors for making a pattern, clay stamps or common household objects for texturing the clay, a nail, tempera paints, brushes and stout string for hanging the pots are needed for this activity.

B. Procedure: Look at the sample weed pot shown in the photograph on page 173. Directions will be easier to follow if you know how the finished product will look.

Roll a clay slab about 3/8 inch thick (see page 158). Cut a paper pattern for an oval approximately 8 inches long by 5 inches wide, 20 by 12.5 cm (or use any other shape desired). Lay the paper pattern on the clay slab. Use a table knife to cut the clay the size of the pattern. Cut the paper pattern in half, crosswise. Use the bottom half as a pattern for cutting a second shape from the clay slab. Cut this shape about 1 inch WIDER than the pattern along each top side, tapering to follow the pattern contour exactly along the bottom edge. This is illustrated in figure 1.

Example:

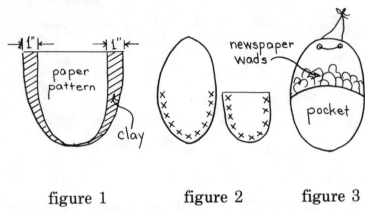

figure 1   figure 2   figure 3

Use clay stamps (see page 164) or other tools to texture this half-oval surface as desired. Allow the two pieces to lie undisturbed about 1/2 hour. Clay should still be moist and flexible, but firm enough not to stretch out of shape when handled.

Score and slip (see page 159) the margins of the lower front surface of the full oval and the back margin of the half oval. These areas are marked with X's in figure 2. Lay the half oval to cover the bottom half of the full oval, scored and slipped sides together and edges aligned. Press the pieces firmly together and reinforce the out-side seam as described on page 159. The half oval, being wider, will stand out to create a pocket. Stuff wadded newspapers into the pocket to hold this shape while the clay dries. Punch two hanging holes along the top edge of the pot (see figure 3).

When the clay is thoroughly dry, brush across all exposed surfaces with dark colored tempera paint. Immediately, wipe across all painted surfaces with a damp paper towel or sponge. The color is now light on smooth, raised surfaces and dark in indentations to accent the textured design. Add a string hanging loop and the pot is ready to hold an arrangement of dried flowers or weeds.

13. OWLS (Shown on page 178, right)

A. Materials: Provide clay, a rolling pin, oilcloth, a table knife, newspaper, masking tape and cylinder-shaped molds (tin cans work well).

B. Procedure: These owls are made from squat, openended cylinders of clay. Roll a clay slab and form a cylinder wall as directed in "Cylinder Pots," page 170. Do not put a base on the cylinder. Let the clay cylinder stand undisturbed, with the mold inside, until the clay dries just enough to hold its shape but is still moist and somewhat pliable.

Remove the center mold. Press two opposite top center edges of the cylinder together to form the top of the owl's head. As you press inward in the center, the outside top edges will spread slightly outward forming ear shapes. Pull outward on the outside top edges to accent the ear shapes. Cut two round holes for eyes. Fasten on bits of clay to form the beak, wings and claws. Score and slip these small pieces (see page 159) and press them firmly into place. Joints on tiny pieces need not be reinforced. Use a toothpick or similar object to scratch feathery textures into the clay.

LEFT: Castles   RIGHT: Owls

When the clay is thoroughly dry, paint the outside surface with dark colored tempera paint. Immediately, use a damp paper towel or sponge to wipe over all painted surfaces. High, smooth areas of clay will now be light colored, with dark coloration remaining in all indentations to accent the texture design.

The two owls pictured on page 178 were glazed and kiln-fired, but were constructed exactly as directed in this activity.

14. CASTLES (Shown on page 178, left)

A. Materials: Students will need clay, a rolling pin, oilcloth, a table knife, tempera paint and brushes.

B. Procedure: When children are experienced in building rectangular pots (see page 166) and cylindrical pots (see page 170), they can combine these skills to make highly imaginative castles.

The basic castle shape is made exactly like a rectangular pot, of whatever size desired. Towers are made from clay cylinders. The cylinders can be open at both ends — no base is needed. Make separate pieces, then join these pieces together to form as simple or intricate a structure as desired. Notched parapet designs can be cut along the top edges of all castle pieces. Use a toothpick or any other similar sharp object to cut stonework patterns or any other detailed features into the clay walls.

When the clay is thoroughly dry, brush over all exposed surfaces with dark colored tempera paint. Immediately, wipe all painted surfaces with a damp paper towel or sponge. Color will now be pale on high, smooth surfaces and dark in indentations to accent etched detailing.

Notice, in the photograph on page 178, the larger castle has a very relaxed construction, giving it an enchanting storybook appearance. The smaller castle is much more formal. There are no "rules" — let each child create according to his own imaginative whim.

SECTION VII "Op Art"

These are designs created to fool the eye: stationary lines vibrate with movement, flat paper bulges, folds or funnels off into space. We "see" what isn't there at all!

The use of hard surfaced paper is stressed in every project using felt pens. Felt pen ink "bleeds" into porous paper making lines fuzzy and ragged. Hard surfaced paper guarantees sharp, crisp lines.

TOP ROW: Repeated Patterns, Something's Wrong
CENTER ROW: Bent Paper Illusion, Positive/Negative Symmetry
BOTTOM ROW: Vanishing Point Illusion, More Bent Paper

1. REPEATED PATTERNS (Shown on page 183, upper left)

A. Materials: Provide hard surfaced paper, a pencil, ruler and a felt pen.

B. Procedure: A whole sheet of paper filled with identical shapes, evenly spaced, appears to vibrate with movement. This is because there is no focal point in a repeated pattern of identical objects. Every part of the picture is as important as every other. With no one spot to hold attention, our eyes move across the design, constantly shifting in search of the non-existing focal point. Soon the pattern itself appears to be dancing.

One simple repeated pattern can be made by filling the paper with evenly spaced lines of identical width. The lines should be spaced very close together. Use a pencil and ruler to mark equal distances along the top and bottom margins of the paper. Use a ruler and felt pen to connect these marks.

Example:

For other all-over patterns, measure and lightly draw pencil lines to divide the paper into even squares. In each square, use a felt pen to color a shape. The shapes can be ovals, rectangles, squares, free-form shapes — any shape at all as long as all shapes on the page are identical and evenly spaced. When the ink is thoroughly dry, erase all penciled guidelines that show.

The photograph on page 183 shows a repeated pattern of triangles. Paper was marked into even squares, then each square was divided in half diagonally. The lower diagonal half of each square was colored black.

2. SOMETHING'S WRONG (Shown on page 183, upper left)

A. Materials: Students will need hard surfaced paper, a pencil, ruler, compass and a felt pen.

B. Procedure: If you really want to fool the eyes, make a repeated pattern as described in "Repeated Patterns," page 184, but incorporate a few "mistakes" for the eyes to discover. This adds even greater visual confusion as the eyes attempt to evaluate the design.

For example, in a straight line design draw a few lines that are wider or narrower than the rest.

Example:

In a pattern of black circles, add a few that are gray or several with a notch cut out. Or, in a pattern of squares, place a few out of alignment.

Example:

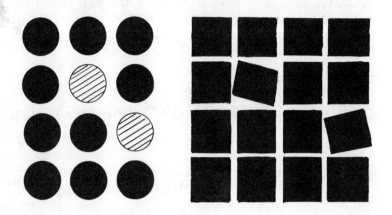

3. BENT PAPER ILLUSION (Shown on page 183, left center)

A. Materials: Hard surfaced paper, a pencil, ruler and a felt pen are needed for this activity.

B. Procedure: Our eyes are amazingly skilled in evaluating perspective and depth. So skilled, in fact, that this kind of design forces them to make a judgement that is totally logical but totally incorrect: it is not the line that has bent, but the paper itself.

Use a ruler and pencil to mark and draw evenly spaced horizontal guidelines across the paper. Keep these lines very light, as some portions will need to be erased. Lightly pencil in several pairs of vertical bars.

Using the ruler to keep all lines perfectly straight, draw in horizontal lines with a felt pen.

Example:

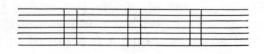

At each set of vertical bars, the lines move at a diagonal to the next higher or lower guidelines.

Example:

Give the ink time to dry thoroughly, then erase all penciled guidelines that show.

Example:

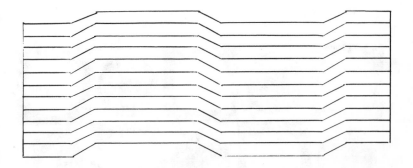

The example shown in the photograph on page 183 is done in this same way, but the vertical bars were curved, not straight. This makes the entire center, oval shaped section of the paper appear to be raised up from the background. Or is it folded down, lower than the background? Can you see it both ways?

4. POSITIVE/NEGATIVE SYMMETRY
(Shown on page 183, center right)

A. Materials: Provide hard surfaced paper, a pencil, ruler, compass and a felt pen.

B. Procedure: The eyes tend to focus on the most important part of a pattern or design. When we present our eyes with two patterns of identical importance, they become confused. Are these white circles on a black background, or black circles on a white background? The eyes see it first one way, then the other. A page full of this type of design soon has our eyes swimming.

To make these designs, pencil in guidelines to divide the paper into many even squares. Draw an identical shape in each square. Use a felt pen to color in the squares, reversing the coloring pattern for foreground and background in neighboring squares.

Example:

C. Variation: The same effect can be achieved with lines. Simply keep the positive space (the black lines) and negative space (the white space between the lines) of identical width. Are these white drawings on black paper, or black drawings on white paper? Can you see them both ways?

Example:

5. VANISHING POINT ILLUSIONS
(Shown on page 183, lower left)

A. Materials: Students will need hard surfaced paper, a pencil, ruler and felt pen.

B. Procedure: These designs make you feel as if you were looking down into a funnel. Converging lines create the illusion of depth. Use a pencil to mark dots along the outside edge of the

Example:

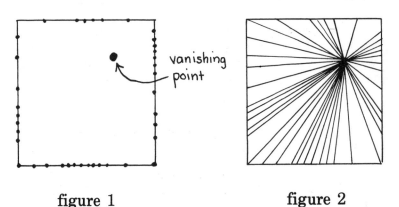

figure 1   figure 2

paper. Space them unevenly, some close together and others farther apart. Anywhere on the paper mark a dot. This dot will be the vanishing point (see figure 1).

Use a ruler and felt pen to connect each mark on the margin of the paper with that vanishing point (see figure 2).

C. Variation: Divide the paper into fourths. In each section, mark evenly spaced marginal dots and a vanishing point. Work each section as previously described and a totally new pattern emerges. The paper appears to be raised up where lines are far apart and goes "down the funnel" at the vanishing point.

Example:

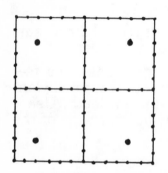 

The example shown in the photograph on page 183 is another variation. Three squares were drawn, one above another. Each square was worked exactly as previously described.

6. MORE BENT PAPER (Shown on page 183, lower right)

A. Materials: Hard surfaced white paper, a pencil, ruler and a black felt pen are needed for this activity.

B. Procedure: Here is another design that makes flat paper appear to fold. Lightly pencil in dots at 1/4-inch intervals along the right and left hand margins of paper. Add vertical lines, slightly slanted, at random intervals across the paper. Mark dots at 1/4-inch intervals along each of these lines (see figure 1).

Example:

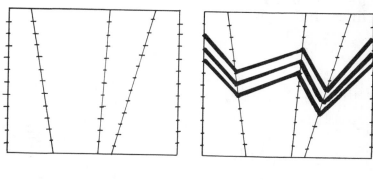

figure 1   figure 2

Connect dots between adjoining bars to create a zigzag pattern across the top of the paper. Continue this pattern, working downward (see figure 2). Work in this way, one row across at a time, until one line touches at the bottom edge of the paper. Finish that row across and the design is complete. Erase all penciled guidelines that show.

7. DISRUPTED LINE DRAWINGS

A. Materials: Provide hard surfaced paper, a pencil, ruler and a felt pen.

B. Procedure: Our eyes expect a line to follow a straight path. When the line suddenly turns in a new direction, our eyes are startled. They do a "double take" to assess what has happened.

To make these eye-startling designs, use penciled lines to divide a paper into fourths. With a pencil, carefully measure and mark evenly spaced guidelines within each of the four sections to create an overall pattern. Trace over these guidelines with a felt pen. When the ink has thoroughly dried, erase all penciled guidelines that show.

Example:

C. Variation: Another type of pattern that produces this same visual "double take" is designs-within-designs. Draw geometric or abstract shapes. Fill in the background with evenly spaced horizontal lines. Fill in the shapes with evenly spaced vertical lines. Wherever possible, let vertical and horizontal lines meet to form crisp 90⁰ angles.

Example:

8. INCOMPLETE DESIGNS

A. Materials: Students will need hard surfaced paper, a pencil, ruler, compass and a felt pen.

B. Procedure: Our eyes tend to see a form as complete, even though a portion is missing. These designs startle the eyes when they discover a gap in a design first conceived to be complete.

To create this illusion, use a pencil to draw the complete design using the compass and ruler as needed. Draw a complete border. Mark off a narrow center section of the design. Use a felt pen to color the complete border (this makes your eyes expect the rest to be complete, too) and all of the design except that narrow center section.

When the ink is thoroughly dry, erase all penciled guidelines that show. On first glance do you notice the gap, or does the design appear complete? Stare at the design and you will "see" the missing portion.

Example:

9. STRIPE VARIATIONS (Shown at the top of page 194)

A. Materials: White hard surfaced paper, a pencil, ruler and colored felt pens are needed for this activity. Use two optically vibrating colors,

TOP: Stripe Vibrations
CENTER: Folded Stripes (2 examples)
BOTTOM ROW: Basket Weave Illusion, Optical Illusion

such as bright red and bright green or bright yellow and bright blue, etc. (See "The Use Of Color In Op Art," page 213.)

B. Procedure: Draw lightly penciled guidelines for horizontal stripes across the paper beginning about 1½ inches down from the top of the paper and ending about 1½ inches from the bottom edge. Stripes should be of greatly varying widths and spaced extremely close together (about 1/16 inch). Color in the stripes using a color combination as previously described. Stripes can alternate colors, or each of the two colors can appear at totally random intervals.

This design is shown in black and white on page 194. It gains an even greater visually vibrating effect in color.

10. FOLDED STRIPE DESIGNS (Shown at center of page 194)

A. Materials: Provide hard surfaced white paper, a pencil, ruler, a black felt pen, white glue and paper on which to mount the completed design.

B. Procedure: Measure and lightly pencil in horizontal lines across the paper. Make some lines close together, others farther apart. Use a black felt pen to trace over these lines. Totally blacken the space between some guidelines to create wide black stripes.

When the ink is thoroughly dry, fold the paper into even vertical accordion pleats. To insure even folds, draw vertical guidelines at 1-1½ inch intervals on the back of the paper. Fold along these lines. Put a few dots of glue here and there along the fold ridges that will touch the mounting sheet. Press the paper onto the mounting sheet and allow the work to lie undisturbed until the glue dries thoroughly.

Or, rather than gluing the pleated paper to a mounting sheet, it can be pinned directly onto the bulletin board for display. Push pins into the fold ridges that touch the board.

11. BASKET WEAVE ILLUSION (Shown on page 194, lower left)

A. Materials: Students will need white hard surfaced paper, a pencil, ruler and a black felt pen.

B. Procedure: Lightly pencil in two sets of five evenly spaced horizontal lines (see figure 1). Add two sets of five evenly spaced vertical lines (see figure 2).

Example:

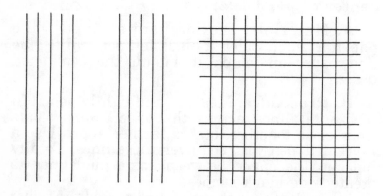

figure 1   figure 2

With a felt pen, draw chevron-shaped lines as shown in figure 3. Count line intersections carefully and exactly duplicate the points where each line begins, turns an angle and ends.

With a felt pen, add vertical lines as shown in figure 4. Notice they stop at each set of horizontal lines and pick up on the opposite side which makes them appear to go under these lines.

Example:

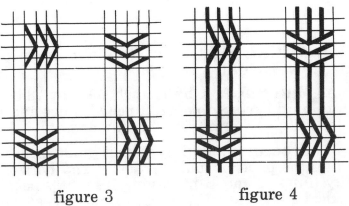

figure 3   figure 4

Use a felt pen to add horizontal lines as shown in figure 5. Erase all penciled guidelines that show. The completed design looks like an over-under basket weave pattern as shown in figure 6. Lines appear to raise up as they cross those running in the opposite direction.

Example:

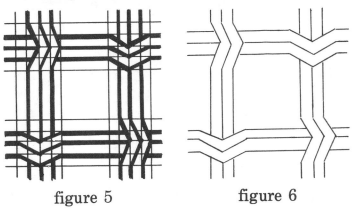

figure 5   figure 6

The example pictured on page 194 was done using the method previously described, but used three sets of nine vertical and horizontal guidelines. There must always be an uneven number of guidelines with five as the minimum number used.

12. OPTICAL ILLUSION (Shown on page 194, lower right)

A. Materials: 8½ by 11 inch (21.5 by 28 cm) white hard surfaced paper, a pencil, ruler and a black felt pen are needed for this activity.

B. Procedure: Lightly pencil guidelines dividing the paper in half vertically and horizontally (lines A and B in figure 1). Lightly pencil vertical guidelines 1½ inches in from each side of the paper (lines C and D in figure 1). With a pencil, draw three lines spaced ½ inch apart along the top and bottom edges of the paper (see figure 2).

Example:

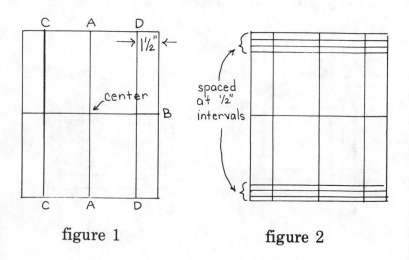

figure 1   figure 2

Along line A, mark dots at ½-inch intervals above the center line (line B) and at 1/4-inch intervals below the center line. Along lines C and D and along right and left margins of the paper, mark dots at 1/4-inch intervals above the center line (line B) and at ½-inch intervals below the center line (see figure 3). Draw pencil lines connecting each row of dots across the sheet (see figure 4).

Example:

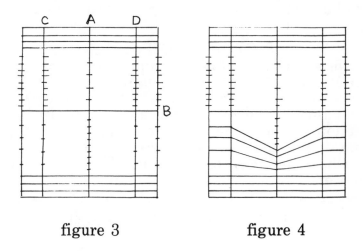

figure 3   figure 4

Use a felt pen to color every other stripe black. Erase all penciled guidelines that show. The resulting design is an optical illusion. Does the center section of the paper look as if it had been folded up? Or does it seem to be folded down? Can you see it both ways?

C. Variation: Instead of black and white, try an optically vibrating color combination. Color the stripes with alternating colors such as bright red and bright green or bright blue and bright green. See "The Use Of Color In Op Art," page 213 for other color scheme ideas.

13. FRACTURED FACES (Shown at top of page 201)

A. Materials: The class will need old magazines, scissors, paste and paper for mounting the completed composition.

B. Procedure: Eerie facial distortions can be made by cutting a picture into pieces, then moving the pieces out of alignment and pasting them in this new position. Two different procedures can be used. Examples constructed by both methods are shown in the photograph on page 201.

SINGLE PICTURE COMPOSITION: Cut out a close-up picture of a face from a magazine. Cut a strip out of the picture. (You may cut away the vertical section showing the center of the face, including the nose, or cut away a horizontal section showing the eyes, etc.) Discard the strip and move the two outer sections together to touch along the center line. The face now appears nose-less, eye-less or minus whatever section was removed from the picture.

TWO PICTURES: Cut two identical close-up face pictures from two copies of the same magazine. Leave one picture whole. Cut the second into two or more pieces. Put the cut pieces on top of the whole picture and shift them into various positions to distort the facial features. Use only one cut piece or several to achieve the desired effect. The face may gain an extra nose, a third eye, an extra set of eyes or a second mouth, etc. Move the pieces into many positions until you achieve the best possible distortion. Try to keep the hairline and chin line in all parts of the overall face design in alignment to heighten the feeling that this is a single unit, not separate pieces. Paste the cut pieces onto the whole pic-

TOP: Fractured Faces (4 examples)
BOTTOM: Split Images (3 examples)

ture. Trim the outer edges of the composition to create an even margin. Paste the picture onto a mounting sheet.

14. SPLIT IMAGES (Shown at bottom of page 201)

A. Materials: Students will need old magazines, scissors, paper for mounting the completed work and rubber cement. Other adhesives could be used, but any smears of rubber cement can be rubbed off which makes the finished work neater.

B. Procedure: Cut two identical close-up face pictures from two issues of the same magazine. (Mark a colored stripe across the back of one picture. While work is in progress, it is easy to confuse which picture is which. The colored stripe is simply an identification mark. Think of the picture with the stripe as Picture A, the picture without the stripe as Picture B.) Cut Picture A in half vertically. This cut should be made in the center of the face, going through the center of the nose. Starting at the center of each half and working outward toward the edges, cut the halves into vertical strips ¼ inch wide. The picture can be ruled into ¼ inch segments on the back side, then cut along these lines for accurately spaced strips. But you must start at the center of each half and measure out from there. Assemble the pieces in proper order at the top of your desk. Move pieces from the left side of the face somewhat apart from the pieces from the right side. The parts from each side are used separately and this arrangement helps cut down confusion of pieces.

Cut Picture B vertically in half, but make this cut about ⅛ inch to the right or left of center.

Then, beginning at the center of each half, measure and cut these pieces into strips ¼ inch wide and assemble the pieces as was done for Picture A. Take the center strip from Picture A and cement it to the center of the mounting sheet. Working on the right side of the face only, take the right center piece from Picture B and paste it against the right side of the strip just pasted. Working progressively towards the right, alternately paste strips from Picture A and Picture B until this side of the face is completed. Begin at the face center and alternately paste strips from the two pictures to complete the left side of the face. The center strip already in place is an "A" piece, so the first piece pasted on this side will be from the "B" picture. The resulting composition has an eerie, out-of-focus appearance.

Here is a work-saving hint. Spread a few lines of rubber cement in the area where strips will be placed. Set each strip into the cement. This is much quicker than applying cement to each individual strip. When the cement has dried, rub off any cement that shows.

C. Variation: Use the same basic procedure and working method for two identical face pictures cut into horizontal strips. Cut Picture A horizontally through the center of the eyes, then work from this point outward to measure and cut the two pieces into strips ¼ inch wide. Cut Picture B in two pieces, with the horizontal cut ⅛ inch above or below that eye-center line. Cut these halves into ¼ inch horizontal strips.

First, paste in place a center strip from Picture A. Paste in place strips taken alternately from Pictures B and A, completing the section above the center, then the section below the center.

15. WAVY WEAVING (Shown on page 205, top row and lower left)

A. Materials: Black construction paper, a pencil, ruler and scissors are needed for this activity. Weaving strips can be cut from such varied materials as colored construction paper, gift wrapping paper, newspaper, burlap, yarn, aluminum foil, ribbon, lace, colored magazine pages, etc.

B. Procedure: Basically, this activity consists of cutting horizontal slits in black construction paper then weaving strips of contrasting materials in and out of these slits. But the manner in which the slits and strips are cut gives this work a strange optical sensation of movement. Slits need not be parallel nor evenly spaced. Weaving strips, too, can be cut in uneven widths or in unusual shapes.

Several examples are pictured on page 205 to give some idea of the wide range of possibilities for creating unusual visual effects using this simple weaving technique. In the upper left example, slits are all parallel, spaced closely together at the top and bottom growing progressively farther apart towards the center. Weaving strips are narrow along each edge growing progressively wider towards the center. The resulting pattern is a woven variation of the "Checkerboard Distortions" described on page 206. The paper appears to bulge up in the center and recede at the edges. In the upper right example, weaving strips (cut from newspaper pages) are of even widths. Slits, however, are wavy and cut at totally random intervals. The resulting pattern gives a strange sensation of undulating movement. In the example shown on the lower left, the slits are cut to widen at the center and grow narrow toward the top and bottom edges of

TOP ROW AND LOWER LEFT: Wavy Weaving
LOWER RIGHT: Checkerboard Distortion

the paper. Weaving strips are blue and white checked ribbon and white lace. The design appears to rise up in the center.

To cut slits that are symmetrical on each side of the paper, fold the black construction paper in half. Measure and mark guidelines for the slits. Cut each slit with scissors, beginning at the center fold and cutting to no closer than ½ inch from the outer edge. Non-symmetrical slits must be cut with the paper opened to full size. Carefully push the scissors tip through the paper, then cut along each penciled guideline.

Encourage children to experiment with a variety of designs in both slits and weaving strips. They may enjoy showing their completed work and telling how slits and strips were designed to achieve various visual effects.

16. CHECKERBOARD DISTORTIONS
(Shown on page 205, lower left)

A. Materials: Provide hard surfaced paper, a pencil, ruler and a felt pen.

B. Procedure: A common checkerboard pattern is produced by drawing evenly spaced horizontal and vertical lines, then coloring every other square black. But if you distort that basic pattern by drawing some horizontal and vertical lines closer together than others and then coloring every other square black, strange things begin to happen.

Our eyes are highly skilled in making perspective judgements. So in evaluating these designs our eyes draw an obvious - and incorrect - conclusion: the larger squares are closer, the smaller squares are farther away. Thus, if larger squares are in the center of the design, that center section appears to bulge up while the edges seem to recede into space. To make this type of design, draw horizontal and vertical guidelines spaced very closely together along each edge of the paper. Space them progressively wider apart toward the center. Then color every other square black.

Example:

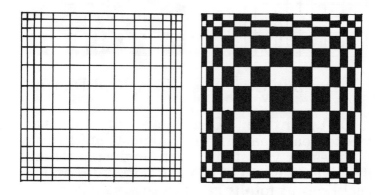

Drawing Grid   Completed Design

The "Checkerboard Distortion" shown in the photograph on page 205 was made by dividing the paper into fourths. Each of the four sections was marked into a grid pattern as previously described, then every other square was colored black. The overall visual effect is impressive indeed.

If the smaller squares are in the center, that center section appears to recede into space while the outer edges appear to bulge upward. To make this type of design, draw horizontal and vertical guidelines spaced far apart along each edge of the paper, growing progressively closer together toward the center.

Example:

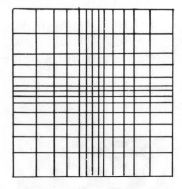

Drawing Grid   Completed Design

C. Variation: Distortions of the basic checkerboard pattern offer almost limitless possibilities for variations, each producing a highly effective design. Try spacing horizontal and vertical lines at totally random intervals (see figure 1). In figure 2, horizontal lines are evenly spaced. Vertical lines widen at the center of the design

Example:

figure 1   figure 2

and grow narrower at the top and bottom margins of the design. In figure 3, vertical lines are straight and evenly spaced, but horizontal lines are wavy and randomly spaced. In figure 4, the vertical bars are narrow towards the center and spread apart at the top and bottom edges.

figure 3   figure 4

Encourage children to experiment with a variety of grid designs to produce unusual visual effects.

17. BULL'S EYE DISTORTIONS

A. Materials: Students will need hard surfaced paper, a pencil, compass, ruler and a felt pen.

B. Procedure: Highly effective, optically confusing designs can be created within a circle. The basic grid is a series of concentric circles like a bull's eye target pattern. Rays are drawn from center to rim. Every other space is colored black. Variations in the spacing between concentric circles and in the spacing between rays produce startling visual effects.

Draw a series of evenly spaced concentric circles. Add rays spaced closely together in some areas, wider apart in others. Color every other space black. The area where rays are closely spaced appears to dip down, while the area of widely spaced rays appears to bulge upward.

Example:

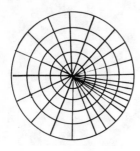

Drawing Grid   Completed Design

If concentric circles are spaced close together in the center, growing progressively more widely spaced on the edges and rays are evenly spaced, the outer edges of the completed design appear raised while the center section goes "down the funnel."

Example:

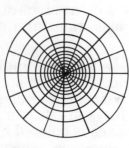

Drawing Grid   Completed Design

If concentric circles are spaced far apart in the center growing progressively closer together towards the edges and rays are evenly spaced, the center section of the design appears to bulge upward while the edges seem to recede into space.

Example:

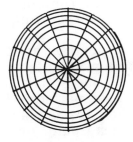
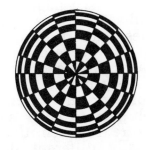

Drawing Grid   Completed Design

Countless other variations of "Bull's Eye Distortion" patterns are possible. Draw a series of concentric circles. Draw straight, jagged or wavy lines cutting through the circles at random intervals. Color every other space black.

Example:

Encourage children to experiment with their own creative variations of "Bull's Eye Distortions."

18. DESIGN WITHIN A DESIGN

A. Materials: Hard surfaced paper, a pencil, ruler, compass and a felt pen are needed for this activity.

B. Procedure: When children are well experienced in creating "Checkerboard Distortions" (see page 206) and "Bull's Eye Distortions" (see page 209), let them combine these skills to create variations incorporating both these pattern designs.

Draw several geometric or abstract shapes on paper. Rule each shape into a grid suitable for a "Checkerboard Distortion," "Bull's Eye Distortion," or any variation of these patterns. Use a felt pen to color every other space black (see figure 1). Then, design a background grid of a totally different design. Blacken every other space in this background design (see figure 2).

Example:

figure 1   figure 2

This procedure offers absolutely limitless creative design possibilities.

19. THE USE OF COLOR IN OP ART

Optical art appears to have a movement of its own, an illusion created by the design itself. All designs are shown in black and white. However, this illusion of movement can be highly reinforced by the use of color in the design.

Some color combinations produce a vibration of their own. Try placing a few bright red squares of paper on a bright green background. Can you see the "vibrations" created solely by this combination of colors? Try combinations of bright yellow with bright blue, or bright orange with bright aqua, or bright green with bright blue. If you use one of these vibrating color combinations for a design which also vibrates, the effect is absolutely amazing.

FOR TEACHER NOTES

FOR TEACHER NOTES

FOR TEACHER NOTES

FOR TEACHER NOTES

DRAMA-PAK™

Each "Pak" contains a playbook for each main
character and one for the director.

SCHOOL FOR ANGELS
A Fantasy · by Natalie Bovee Hutson
Six Main Characters

Less than one week until Christmas and chaos reigns in The Gre
Beyond! While Earth bombards the Heavenly Headmaster with urge
requests for "perfect" angels, it is discovered that the current "croj
is woefully lacking in "angel skills". Cherubs have been playii
frisbee with the stars, conducting pillow fights with the clouds, ai
swinging from the Pearly Gates. The angel choir doesn't even knc
the words to "Silent Night"!

A delightful play for all ages and all seasons.

☐ **304-7** **$9.9**

THE GRUMBLE GROUP
A Comedy · by Natalie Bovee Hutson
Five Characters

The Grumble Group meets regularly (and grudgingly) at a city b
stop, where they find endless subjects about which to complain. (
the surface these four individuals appear to be cantankerous old-timer
finding nothing right with the world. But as they reveal themselves
the audience, and through the help of an optimistic newcomer,
slowly becomes apparent that beneath the somewhat comic exterioi
lie sensitive people who have, for various reasons, become quite d
enchanted with life.

A good choice for all ages.

☐ **301-2** **$9.9**

ME, BETH CONNORS
A Teenage Drama · by Natalie Bovee Hutson
Seven Characters

Meet Beth Connors, an average twelve-year-old, who through
series of flashbacks, takes the audience by the hand and leads the
through a typical day in her life. It's a day filled with girlish gigglin
a mysterious phone call, and the usual scraps with a pesky young
brother. But best of all, it is a day in which a routine visit to h
grandmother in a nursing home, enables Beth to view life in a mo
adult manner.

☐ **303-9** **$9.9**

DRAMA-PAK™

Each "Pak" contains a playbook for each main characters and one for the director.

MR. TEDLEY'S TREEHOUSE
A Drama for the Young · by Natalie Bovee Hutson
Seven Characters

Mr. Tedley is a child's dream come true. He lives alone in a treehouse surviving on berries and nuts, offering friendship and vast knowledge to the younger set. But is he real? Ryan and Joey know that he is, but cannot convince others of the fact, and this troubles them.

In a simplistic way, the play deals with every child's need to fantasize and cling to dreams. Yet it also emphasizes that there comes a time when one must leave the fantasies behind and face the real world.

A charming play for young and old.

☐ 302-0...$9.95

THE READING OF THE WILL
A Farce · by Natalie Bovee Hutson
Seven Characters

Henry P. Jaybody may be deceased, but he is not absent from the reading of his will! Knowing that his greedy heirs would do their best to "out-mourn" each other, Henry had the foresight to plan a scene which would send the tribe in all directions, showing their true colors - and practically trampling one another in the process.

An action-filled play with characters who are fun to portray and even funnier to watch.

☐ 305-5...$9.95

THE WRONGFUL CLAIM
An Old-Fashioned Melodrama · by Natalie Bovee Hutson
Eight Characters

The lovely and innocent Melody Lark is but a servant in the home of wealthy Vanessa Vapors. Vanessa's avaricious daughter, Crystal, is envious of Melody's childlike charm and attentions of the gardener, Barnaby Barnhart. So when Crystal accidentally discovers that Melody is about to fall heir to a fortune, she plots her disinheritance. Unaware of his sister's scheme, an equally greedy Humphrey Vapors devises his own plot to discredit Melody.

An old-fashioned melodrama with lots of heroes and villains and a chance to hiss, boo, and applaud them all.

☐ 300-4...$9.95

TABLETMASTERS™

Duplicator Masters You Tear from a Tablet!

and only.......

$3^{95} each

- Faster to Use
- Easier to Handle
- Flat-Stacking

Factual Recall

Description	Grade	Cat. No.
Helps the student make use of pictures and words in a fact-finding experience, using detailed recall and supportive visual evidence. Excellent diagnostic tool for determining comprehension and ability to relate observation to written questions.	1	603-8
	2	607-0
	3	611-9

Following Directions

Description	Grade	Cat. No.
Provides realistic drills necessary to teach students the processes of reading, understanding, and then following directions. Each worksheet has a number of directions, each of which must be completed progressively. Verbal instructions may be added.	1	604-6
	2	608-9
	3	612-7

Thinking Skills

Description	Grade	Cat. No.
Study sheets call for visual sequencing, reasoning, classifying, and using cause and effect thinking skills. Sharpens each student's ability to draw conclusions, and their reasoning should be explained before answers are accepted or rejected.	1	605-4
	2	609-7
	3	613-5

Vocabulary Development

Description	Grade	Cat. No.
Promotes word-building through usage, exploration, similarities, expressive language and identification. Matching pictures and words reinforces the relationship between the two. A range of descriptive words, synonyms, antonyms and other forms is used.	1	606-2
	2	610-0
	3	614-3

DUPLICATOR BOOKS

Use our ideas in duplicator form to cut teacher preparation time and fulfill the needs for supplementary activities in the following areas of study:

LANGUAGE ARTS

- ☐ **ED501-5 SPICE VOL. I** — K-2
- ☐ **ED502-3 SPICE VOL. II** — 2-4
- ☐ **ED505-8 ANCHOR VOL. I** — 4-6
- ☐ **ED506-6 ANCHOR VOL. II** — 6-8
- ☐ **ED564-3 PHONICS VOL. I** — K-2
- ☐ **ED565-1 PHONICS VOL. II** — 2-4
- ☐ **ED567-8 GRAMMAR VOL. I** — 4-6
- ☐ **ED568-6 GRAMMAR VOL. II** — 6-8
- ☐ **ED509-0 RESCUE VOL. I** — K-4
  (Remedial Reading)
- ☐ **ED516-3 FLAIR VOL. I** — 3-8
  (Creative Writing)
- ☐ **ED527-9 DICTIONARY VOL. I** — K-2
  (Single Letters)
- ☐ **ED528-7 DICTIONARY VOL. II** — K-2
  (Blends)
- ☐ **ED529-5 DICTIONARY VOL. III** — 3-6
- ☐ **ED530-9 DICTIONARY VOL. IV** — 7-9
- ☐ **ED537-6 LIBRARY VOL. I** — 3-6
- ☐ **ED538-4 LIBRARY VOL. II** — 7-9

MUSIC

- ☐ **ED561-9 NOTE VOL. I** — K-2
- ☐ **ED562-7 NOTE VOL. II** — 3-6

SAFETY

- ☐ **ED519-8 PREVENT VOL. I** — K-4
- ☐ **ED520-1 PREVENT VOL. II** — 4-8

ONLY $6⁹⁵ Each

EARLY LEARNING

- ☐ **ED512-0 LAUNCH VOL. I**
  (Basic Readiness)
- ☐ **ED513-9 LAUNCH VOL. II**
  (Additional Skills)

MATHEMATICS

- ☐ **ED533-3 PLUS VOL. I** — K-2
- ☐ **ED534-1 PLUS VOL. II** — 2-4
- ☐ **ED523-6 CHALLENGE VOL. I** — 4-6
- ☐ **ED524-4 CHALLENGE VOL. II** — 6-8

SCIENCE

- ☐ **ED546-5 PROBE VOL. I** — K-2
- ☐ **ED547-3 PROBE VOL. II** — 2-4
- ☐ **ED550-3 INQUIRE VOL. I** — 4-8

SOCIAL STUDIES

- ☐ **ED553-8 SPARK VOL. I** — K-2
- ☐ **ED554-6 SPARK VOL. II** — 2-4
- ☐ **ED557-0 FOCUS VOL. I** — 4-6
- ☐ **ED558-9 FOCUS VOL. II** — 6-8

* *

ONLY $4⁵⁰ Each

EXCLUSIVE WORD LISTS
Each book contains a graded word list — from 738 words at Level 1 to 4,325 words at Level 6.

"Work with Words" Duplicator Books Develop and Reinforce Language Skills on 6 Levels!

A creative new series from the publishers of Spice! Here's a fresh and dynamic approach to teaching and reinforcing language skills. Each master is clearly identified as to the learning objective: recognizing sounds, visual identification, word recognition, word usage, spelling, alphabetizing, word meaning, and so on. Thus the teacher can locate just the right activity at just the right time! To top if off, each book contains our exclusive and previously unpublished graded word list for that level. Each 8½ × 11" book has teacher's guide; 20 masters. Use with any basal program to extend learning through skill-building activities.

☐ **ED262-8** Level 1A	738 words		☐ **ED268-7** Level 4A	2970 words
☐ **ED263-6** Level 1B	738 words		☐ **ED269-5** Level 4B	2970 words
☐ **ED264-4** Level 2A	1416 words		☐ **ED270-9** Level 5A	3613 words
☐ **ED265-2** Level 2B	1416 words		☐ **ED271-7** Level 5B	3613 words
☐ **ED266-0** Level 3A	2303 words		☐ **ED272-5** Level 6A	4325 words
☐ **ED267-9** Level 3B	2303 words		☐ **ED273-3** Level 6B	4325 words

☐ **WWP-500** Complete Set of all 12 books above $54.00

Note: "B" level books are slightly more advanced than "A" level.

Duplicators and idea-books (shown on opposite side) are available at the leading school supply dealers. Ask for them by name.

For a current catalog, contact the publisher.

80484

IDEA-BOOKS FOR ELEMENTARY SCHOOL TEACHERS

Each book was created to meet teachers' needs for simple and explicit ideas to enrich the many subject areas presented to their students.

ONLY **$6⁹⁵** Each

LANGUAGE ARTS

- ☐ **ED101-X SPICE** — Primary Language Arts ● Grades K-4
- ☐ **ED109-5 ANCHOR** — Intermediate Language Arts ● Grades 4-8
- ☐ **ED128-1 RESCUE** — Primary Remedial Reading ● Grades K-4
- ☐ **ED112-5 FLAIR** — Creative Writing ● Grades K-8
- ☐ **ED122-2 SCRIBE** — Handwriting ● Grades K-8
- ☐ **ED126-5 PRESS** — Newspaper Activities ● Grades K-8
- ☐ **ED130-3 PHONICS** — Primary Phonics ● Grades K-4
- ☐ **ED134-6 GRAMMAR** — Intermediate Grammar ● Grades 4-8
- ☐ **ED131-1 LISTEN** — Listening Activities ● Grades K-8
- ☐ **ED133-8 VIDEO** — Television Activities ● Grades K-8
- ☐ **ED136-2 REFLECT** — Creative Thought ● Grades 4-Adult
- ☐ **ED137-0 VALUES** — Values Clarification ● Grades K-8
- ☐ **ED139-7 KID'S LIT** — Reading Through Lit ● Grades K-8
- ☐ **ED141-9 LIB. STUDIES** — Library Skills ● Grades K-9

MATHEMATICS & SCIENCE

- ☐ **ED103-6 PLUS** — Primary Mathematics ● Grade K-4
- ☐ **ED116-8 CHALLENGE** — Intermediate Mathematics ● Grades 4-8
- ☐ **ED118-4 METER** — Metrics ● Grades K-8
- ☐ **ED102-8 PROBE** — Primary Science ● Grades K-4
- ☐ **ED121-4 INQUIRE** — Intermediate Science ● Grades 4-8
- ☐ **ED140-0 NATURE** — Outdoor Education ● Grades K-8

SOCIAL STUDIES

- ☐ **ED104-4 SPARK** — Primary Social Studies ● Grades K-4
- ☐ **ED125-7 FOCUS** — Intermediate Social Studies ● Grades 4-8
- ☐ **ED120-6 CHOICE** — Economics ● Grades K-8
- ☐ **ED123-0 CAREER** — Career Education ● Grades K-8
- ☐ **ED135-4 COMPASS** — Map Skills ● Grades K-8

SPECIALTY STUDIES

- ☐ **ED111-7 LAUNCH** — Preschool and Kindergarten Readiness
- ☐ **ED127-3 HOLIDAY** — Holiday Art ● Grades K-8
- ☐ **ED105-2 CREATE** — Primary Art ● Grades K-4
- ☐ **ED124-9 CRAFT** — Intermediate Art ● Grades 4-8
- ☐ **ED113-3 NOTE** — Music ● Grades K-8
- ☐ **ED119-2 GROWTH** — Health ● Grades K-8
- ☐ **ED115-X PREVENT** — Safety ● Grades K-8
- ☐ **ED107-9 STAGE** — Dramatics ● Grades K-8
- ☐ **ED106-0 ACTION** — Physical Education ● Grades K-6
- ☐ **ED117-6 DISPLAY** — Bulletin Board Ideas

Address: ☐ Home ☐ School (Preferred)

Name _____

Address _____

_____

City _____ State _____ Zip _____

Idea-books and duplicators (shown on the opposite side) are available at leading school supply dealers or Educational Service, Inc., PO Box 219, Stevensville, Michigan 49127 **1-800-253-0763.**

82586